CHANGING PATTERNS IN CHRISTIAN EDUCATION

CHANGING PATTERNS

IN CHRISTIAN EDUCATION

Marshall C. Dendy

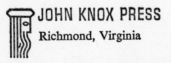 JOHN KNOX PRESS
Richmond, Virginia

Scripture quotations from the Revised Standard Version are copyright 1946 and 1952 by the National Council of the Churches of Christ in the United States of America.

LIBRARY OF CONGRESS CATALOG CARD NUMBER: 65-10715

© M. E. BRATCHER 1964

PRINTED IN THE UNITED STATES OF AMERICA

2371(WB)7365

Dedicated to
Nan
who has helped me understand
the wonder of a covenant

Preface

The faculty of Columbia Theological Seminary of Decatur, Georgia, my alma mater, invited me to deliver the Alumni Lectures to be presented in November 1963. The invitation indicated that the lectures could be prepared on a subject of my choosing but suggested that in view of my position as Executive Secretary for the Board of Christian Education of the Presbyterian Church in the United States it would be appropriate to develop a theme in the field of Christian education.

Since the Board was developing the Covenant Life Curriculum, it occurred to me that a study of the works and ministries of John Calvin and John Knox, two of the great Reformers, might shed some light on the general subject of Christian education. Were the Reformers interested in instructing the members of their congregations? If so, what concepts of Christian education were reflected in their ministry? Could it be that the principles upon which a new curriculum of Christian education is being developed in the middle of the twentieth century had their roots in the works of men who lived four hundred years ago?

The study resulted in the material found in the lectures presented to the faculty and students of Columbia Seminary. The author is greatly indebted to the President of the Seminary, Dr. J. McDowell Richards, the faculty members, and the members of the student body for their encouragement to produce the lectures in permanent form. Members of the staff of John Knox Press gave invaluable assistance to the author while the manuscript was being prepared for publication, and Miss Susan L. Lewman, Director of Christian Education of the First Presbyterian Church of Orlando, Florida, when the author was pastor there but now an employee of the Board, has gone the "extra mile" in typing the material.

It is the hope of the author that these studies may give further assurance of the importance of Christian education and the trustworthiness of the strong foundation upon which the Covenant Life Curriculum has been developed.

Marshall C. Dendy

CONTENTS

1 | HISTORY IS PROLOGUE

Christian education is an extremely important part of the work of the church. The church is called to preach and teach the gospel. Jesus called twelve men to become his disciples. They were commissioned to go into all the world and make disciples of all the nations, "teaching them to observe all that I have commanded you" (Matthew 28:20, R.S.V.). But prior to the hour they were given this commission they spent three years at the feet of the greatest Teacher who ever lived. They were taught the meaning of prophecies that foretold the coming of the Messiah. They were instructed in the nature of life of those who are citizens of the "kingdom of heaven" (Matthew 5-7). They learned that "the Son of man must suffer many things, and be rejected by the elders and the chief priests and the scribes, and be killed, and after three days rise again" (Mark 8:31, R.S.V.). They learned of Christ by living in his company as well as by listening when he expounded the mysteries of the kingdom of God. After the coming of the Holy Spirit they preached and taught with a power that startled their hearers.

The church has been preaching and teaching the gospel ever since. The specific purposes of teaching have changed as conditions changed. Converts to Christianity coming out of a pagan culture required specific instruction in the nature of the faith they embraced. They were taught to renounce the old beliefs as well as to accept the new faith. The essential elements of the Christian faith were soon summarized and are clearly stated in the Apostles' Creed. They are a part of the heritage of the church.

After the days of Constantine, when great masses of the people of the Roman Empire became nominal Christians, the church be-

11

gan to emphasize the importance of teaching children and youth the doctrines of the faith. It was only after intensive instruction in the Creed and related beliefs of the church that young people were accepted as members who could participate in the Lord's Supper.

The forms and objectives of Christian education have shifted through the years. At times the church has placed great emphasis upon the importance of catechetical instruction. During the Dark Ages, when few people could read and many priests were illiterate, instruction in the stories of the Bible was offered through pictures and various other forms of art that could be seen. There have been times when the church failed to take seriously the education of her people. But there has never been a time, nor will there be one, when the church has been released from the responsibility of teaching the Word of God.

During the twentieth century there has been a remarkable growth in Christian education in the Protestant churches of the United States and Canada. This is reflected in many ways. The growth in the enrollment of members in church schools and youth organizations has been greater than at any other period of time. Professionally trained directors of Christian education are required to assist pastors in their ministry. Since 1950, churches in the United States have invested annually a billion and a half dollars in the construction of buildings for the program of Christian education. Millions of volunteer church school teachers devote their time to the teaching of children and youth. More recently, adults in great numbers have been enrolled in the work of the church school. Boards of Christian Education have been created by many denominations to plan a curriculum of Christian education and to produce appropriate materials for their educational program.

Although Christian education has made a valuable contribution to the development of the church, the time has come for it to be critically examined and evaluated. Has the success of Christian education been exaggerated? Why, with the enrollment of so many young people in the organized program of the church, is there the prevalence of delinquency and the great increase of crime among American youth? Why do young people drop out of church school at the very age when they need religious instruction most? Is the church school providing a quality of instruction that can be re-garded as truly educational?

Within recent years many of our theologians and an increasing number of pastors have been concerned about the basic principles upon which Christian education has been developed. They have come to the scene quite late. Ever since the modern Sunday school movement began in 1781, as a result of the interest Robert Raikes had in offering instruction to ignorant and underprivileged children, theologians and ministers have left to the laity the re-sponsibility of teaching in the church school. The laity found in the Sunday school movement opportunities for service in the name of Christ. This in itself was good for the church and particularly for the laymen who devoted their time to this work. But as laymen were not as thoroughly trained in theology as were the clergy, many clergymen were not only suspicious of a movement in which the laity predominated but actually opposed the Sunday school movement. They thought children and youth would be misled by those who were not well grounded in the theological disciplines of the church.

Christian education in Protestant churches in the early part of the twentieth century was developed in large measure by educa-tors rather than by theologians and biblical scholars. Thus the movement at that time reflected educational concepts of public school education. Many of these concepts are valuable. To under-stand how learning takes place, to know the nature of a child and the child's interests and capacities, and to recognize the social con-ditions in which a generation is being educated are essential con-siderations for those who develop a curriculum and for those who teach.

For the past fifteen or twenty years Christian education has been under the critical eye of the church. Theologians and pastors have become aware of the importance of the purpose of Christian education and the content of materials used in the educational program of the church. Boards of Christian Education have taken the initiative in creating curricula of Christian education based on sound biblical interpretation and reflecting new insights in theol-ogy. Development in social sciences has provided educators with a deeper understanding of man, of human behavior, of group behavior, and of how learning takes place. New media of communication are available for education. The exploration of space has forced man to think in new dimensions. Yet Christian education has not sufficiently challenged children and youth. New curricula of Christian education for all ages are being created by most of the Protestant denominations in the United States and Canada.

It appears at this time that the latter part of the twentieth century will be characterized by the most remarkable development in science, communications, and learning techniques of any similar period of history. Christian education has developed more rapidly in this century than in any other period of the church's history. Are the concepts of Christian education reflected in the new curricula valid? Are they new concepts? Are the principles that underlie the educational programs of this century biblical? One reason history is studied is that there is much to be learned from those who lived in past centuries. No generation, regardless of its development, has a monopoly on knowledge and wisdom. Indeed, in the field of religion and ethics man in the twentieth century can hardly be regarded as excelling those who lived in other centuries. The Renaissance and the Protestant Reformation were periods when men broke out of narrow forms of knowledge, theology, and ethics.

In the Reformed Churches, more commonly known in this country as Presbyterian, two of the most influential theologians and Reformers were John Calvin and John Knox. They were effective preachers and fearless men who changed the course of history. Calvin was a theologian of the highest order, and Knox was a militant churchman. Both men were aware of the importance of education. Both championed the education of the masses. Both promoted sound instruction in the faith. Since they achieved great success in their role as leaders, since they placed such great emphasis upon instruction in the faith, and since the church under their guidance experienced a genuine reform, it would be well to discover the concepts of Christian nurture reflected in their writings and works. It is possible that the concepts reflected in the development of Christian education today can be tested or evaluated in the light of the concepts found productive in the ministry of Calvin and Knox.

2 | CALVIN AND CHRISTIAN EDUCATION

John Calvin has won his place in history. He has influenced the culture, government, and theology of Western civilization. His theology, particularly as it is found in the *Institutes of the Christian Religion,* has gained recognition throughout the world. Calvin was a courageous and bold reformer. He was a preacher of just fame, drawing to Geneva scholars, teachers, and preachers from the nations of Europe. They eagerly sought to learn the doctrines Calvin expounded from the Bible, doctrines which resulted in reformation in both church and state. Central in Calvin's writings and ministry was the emphasis he placed upon teaching. What he taught shook the foundations of empires and of the church.

The revolutionary nature of Calvin's teachings can be understood only in the context of the age in which he lived. The Renaissance was well advanced. Feudalism was being supplanted by strong, centralized governments. There was a new birth of learning. While the masses of people were uneducated and illiterate, as were the vast majority of those who were in positions of leadership in church and state, the darkness of the night was beginning to fade. Students were seeking an education. A few men whose minds had found freedom as truth liberated them from error began to speak, write, and teach. They met the challenge of their age with minds and hearts prepared to attack error and wrong. They were eager to lay the foundations for an order of society based upon truth and reason inspired and enlightened by revelation.

John Calvin was born in Noyon, France, on July 10, 1509. His father, Gérard, was a notary, skilled in legal and administrative business. He was ambitious for his son and secured benefices from the church for his son's education. When John Calvin was not quite twelve years of age, his father secured his appointment as chaplain of a cathedral. This office provided funds for his education, but the duties were only nominally assumed and were performed by others for a small sum. John Calvin's mother, Jeanne Lefranc, the daughter of an innkeeper, was known for her piety and beauty. She died when John was only about three years of age.

The brilliance of Calvin's mind was evidenced early in his career as a student. At the age of fourteen he entered the University of Paris, where his instructors regarded him as precocious, a judgment fully substantiated by his scholarly achievements. His genius was recognized also at Orléans. While a student there he was invited by an instructor to lecture to the students in his absence, a practice unheard of in that day. As a youth Calvin was a strict censor of everything, vicious in his condemnation of the conduct of his companions. Calvin's learning habits are noteworthy. He read intensively and each morning meditated upon the things he had read the previous evening, storing in his phenomenal memory passages and truths encountered in his readings. He had a thorough knowledge of Hebrew, Greek, and Latin, and mastered the writings of the church fathers. His knowledge of French enabled him to speak and write with a clarity and conciseness unrivaled in his day or since. One of his contemporaries stated that when Calvin was only twenty-two years of age he was the best educated man in Europe.

The revolutionary nature of Calvin's views was evident when he was in his early twenties. In 1533 his friend Nicolas Cop was elected rector of the University of Paris. In the inaugural address, delivered by custom on All Saints' Day, errors of Catholicism were attacked boldly and incisively. Calvin was known to hold similar views, and because of his supposed association with the radical address he was compelled to flee from Paris. He found refuge in a distant part of France, among people who accepted the Reformation teachings advanced by the young theologian. It was during this period that Calvin drafted the outlines of the Institutes. He dedicated the Institutes to the "Most Mighty and Illustrious Monarch, Francis, Most Christian King of the French." Referring to the king as his sovereign, Calvin wished him "Peace and Salvation in Christ."[1] It was a bold act, typical of Calvin's writings to sovereigns of European nations.

As the Reformation spread in France, Calvin, well known as a leader of the new movement, had to seek safety abroad. He went to Strasbourg, where the Reformation was flourishing, and then found a quiet refuge in Basel. After completing his Institutes and arranging for their publication, he journeyed to Ferrara in Italy, to visit the Duchess of Ferrara, a sister to Francis I and friendly to the Reformation. From there he set out for Strasbourg, but normal routes were closed by the wars and he had to go by way of Geneva. William Farel, the fiery Reformer and a fellow Frenchman, learned of Calvin's presence in that city. He sought out Calvin and engaged him in one of the memorable interviews of history. He invited Calvin to remain in Geneva and there to organize the Reformation along the lines of the Institutes. Calvin, who was eager to go to Strasbourg and continue his studies, was unwilling to accept Farel's invitation, whereupon Farel said, "I denounce unto you, in the name of Almighty God, that if, under the pretext of prosecuting your studies, you refuse to labour with us in this work of the Lord, the Lord will curse you, as seeking yourself rather than Christ."[2] It was strong language, not the kind usually heard when men receive calls to the ministry. But the words of Farel moved Calvin. Terrified by the denunciation, he accepted the invitation and remained in Geneva.

Thus there was begun, in 1536, the work of Calvin in the city that would thereafter be associated with the name and writings of the greatest theologian of the day. Indeed, Calvin is regarded by many as the greatest theologian since Augustine. He sought reform in government. He drew up plans for the organization of the City Council. He pleaded for moral reform in a city where there was licentiousness, profanity, bawdy songs, degraded entertainment, adultery, political intrigues, and injustices of every kind. There came a time when opposition to his leadership and moral demands was so great that Calvin was rejected by the City Council. He left Geneva for Strasbourg, so low in funds that he had to sell many of his books in order to purchase food.

Conditions in Geneva grew steadily worse after Calvin's departure. The young Reformer was urged to return and to continue the reformation he had begun. It was only after repeated invitations from Geneva that Calvin left the Strasbourg he loved and returned to Geneva in 1541. Calvin believed God had called him, and he felt that he should return and labor in Christ's name in the city from which he had fled but which offered such promise for the work close to his heart. There he spent the remaining years of his life. Those years were filled with strife, opposition, and personal insults by citizens who resisted the reforms he instituted. But Calvin persistently advanced his views, worked with the City Council, and succeeded in bringing about a genuine reformation in the city. John Knox, who spent some years with Calvin, regarded Geneva as the most Christian community he had ever seen.

As one reads Calvin's *Institutes of the Christian Religion,* his commentaries, and the other writings of this brilliant, indefatigable scholar, preacher, and teacher, certain principles and doctrines of a fundamental nature are apparent. These reflect Calvin's concepts of Christian nurture. It would be erroneous to conclude that John Calvin was engaged in a ministry of Christian education after the patterns of the twentieth century. The forms and activities of Christian education today are, in many instances, clearly unlike those found in the ministry of Calvin. But there are some concepts of Christian education reflected in Calvin's writings and ministry which were not only noteworthy for his day but are of profound value to those who, in any day, are concerned about the way the Christian faith is understood and taught. Christian education as understood by Calvin is the use of a body of truth concerning the Christian faith, essentially the revealed Word of God, by the believing community, in reliance upon the work of the Holy Spirit, so that men may be confronted by God, believe in Christ, be informed concerning the great beliefs of the Christian Church, and be rightly related to God and man.

Emphasis Upon the Scriptures

Basic in the life and works of John Calvin is the place of the Word of God. The doctrine of the Scriptures clearly set forth in his ministry and writings is one of the keys to an understanding of his work as a Reformer and of his abiding influence. The Bible is unique in that it offers man knowledge of God to be found in no other source save the Word Incarnate. This is stated in the Institutes as follows: ". . . since we are not favoured with daily oracles from heaven, and since it is only in the Scriptures that the Lord hath been pleased to preserve his truth in perpetual remembrance, it obtains the same complete credit and authority with believers, when they are satisfied of its divine origin, as if they heard the very words pronounced by God himself."[3] Calvin regarded the Scriptures as an instrument or means whereby God himself spoke to man. The Scriptures constitute a *living* book. What is written and understood is not simply truth about God but is a word whereby God addresses himself to man.

The nature of the divine origin and authority of the Bible as Calvin understood it is summarized in the following passages:

"It must be maintained, as I have before asserted, that we are not established in the belief of the doctrine till we are indubitably persuaded that God is its Author. . . . Now . . . this persuasion must be sought from a higher source than human reasons, or judgments, or conjectures—even from the secret testimony of the Spirit."[4] "The testimony of the Spirit is superior to all reason. For as God alone is a sufficient witness of himself in his own word, so also the word will never gain credit in the hearts of men, till it be confirmed by the internal testimony of the Spirit."[5]

Calvin's belief in the primacy of the authority of the Word of God must be viewed in the light of the historic belief in the primacy of the authority of the church through popes and councils. The Reformers refused to accept as infallible the authority of men, individually or collectively, however pious they might be. Man can and does err. Church councils or courts do not possess, and were not promised, infallible wisdom. Therefore, the Reformers wrote, proclaimed, and taught that they would take their stand upon the truths set forth in the Word of God as the Word was illumined by the Holy Spirit. Luther and Calvin both declared emphatically that wherein and wherever the traditions and teachings of men were in conflict with the teachings of the Scriptures they must be rejected. Thus Calvin encouraged the most serious, diligent, and prayerful study of the Scriptures, that men might discern for themselves the authority and meaning of the Word of God.

Calvin's views concerning the relation of the church to Scripture are important. He taught that the church was established on the basis of revelation and that its guidance is to be found in a true understanding of the Bible. "If the Church was given existence through the agency of the Scriptures, it was itself a proof of their source and origin; the divine power in the Church witnessed to the divine power of the Word."[6] Calvin taught that "The Scriptures were not really the Word of God to any one, whatever his professed belief, unless they did the sanctifying work of God on mind and heart."[7] As the church was brought into existence through revelation, its very existence is evidence of God's activity and initiative in calling into being the believing community.

The preaching of this great Reformer was primarily the exposition of the Word of God. His was a teaching ministry. He brought to his study of the Scriptures a new approach, a viewpoint which is as foundational today as it was revolutionary then. He believed that God was speaking to man through the Word, that the Bible is a living Word, and that in the Word is a call to man to believe, to live, and to glorify God. The realization that one may and indeed does come into encounter with God when the Scriptures are heard and understood makes the teaching and hearing of them significant and exciting.

Another of Calvin's revolutionary views was his emphasis upon the trustworthiness of the interpretation of the Bible by those who came to it with a sympathetic viewpoint. The Bible was to be understood through "the appreciative understanding of the principles animating the characters appearing in it or determining the situation presented."[8] This is a viewpoint which gained deliverance for the reader from the then prevalent view of Rome, that the Bible could be interpreted only by those who were skilled in the use of allegorical interpretations of the Scriptures, or who possessed the knowledge reflected in tradition. Of Calvin's revolutionary method of Bible study, Bungener wrote: "It is good sense dethroning scholastic erudition; and it is truth, sought in every verse, and every word, by the straightest and shortest road."[9]

To the necessity for a sympathetic viewpoint Calvin added another principle of sound interpretation of the Bible. The Bible was to be interpreted in the light of the entire message it contains. He knew that there is unity in the Scriptures and that any interpreter who would violate this unity would err. If there is a passage of Scripture that appears to be out of harmony with the larger truth of the Bible, that particular passage must be studied more carefully to discern what was in the mind of the writer. As clear and simple as this principle appears today, it corrected a practice common in Calvin's day—that of lifting a verse or passage out of context and giving it a meaning the writer did not intend it to have.

Calvin brought to the interpretation of the Bible the skill, equipment, and industry of the scholar. He was a brilliant student of Hebrew, Greek, and Latin. He knew the value of the shades of meaning the original language gave to the text. He possessed an uncanny knowledge of the usage of words in the various periods during which the Bible was written. His commentaries have stood the test of the centuries. They are recognized by scholars today as works that shed true light upon the meaning of the language and the message of the Scriptures.

Pastors were encouraged to study the Scriptures. Few priests could read the original languages in which the Bible was written. Calvin knew the ministers of the church would never be able to proclaim and teach the gospel with all of its implications unless they were genuine students and exegetes. Calvin encouraged the pastors of Geneva to meet one day in the week for the express purpose of studying the Bible, gaining insights from one another as pastors commented upon interpretations given by fellow pastors. It was a good discipline. Such studies encouraged diligence and honesty on the part of ministers. They learned from one another, and undoubtedly the custom produced humility of spirit in those whose interpretations were reviewed. It also required a spirit of fairness on the part of the critics. Modern methods of group study are not so modern after all.

The edification of adults was emphasized by the Geneva Reformer. That Calvin encouraged the daily reading and study of the Bible by adults is indicated in the following passage from the *Catechism of the Church of Geneva*: ". . . every one ought to exercise himself in the daily reading of it, and all should be especially careful to attend the sermons when the doctrine of salvation is expounded in the assembly of the faithful."[10] The passage continues: "It is little to have begun, unless you persevere. We must be the disciples of Christ to the end, or rather without end. But he has committed to the ministers of the Church the office of teaching in his name and stead."[11]

Such concepts are significant. The Bible is to be read and understood by the masses of people. It is not to be restricted in its use. Its meaning can be understood by one who approaches it with humility. The Bible lends itself to common-sense understanding and interpretation. Scholarly, diligent study by pastors and teachers is demanded. The truth of the Bible lies in its Source: it is an inspired book. In the knowledge of God and of man's relationship to God and man, revelation takes precedence over logic. These concepts were revolutionary. The danger of placing the Bible in the hands of the untutored and unordained was repeatedly emphasized by the Roman hierarchy. Individual interpretations could lead to division in the church, to heresy, and to error. But this very principle of having the Scriptures read and studied by all Christians was one of the strengthening elements of the Reformation. Men heard God speak through the Bible. They found there authority for truth and for guidance. The Scriptures illumined by the Holy Spirit became the source of authority for the church.

Emphasis Upon Instruction in Theology

A second characteristic of Calvin's teachings was the emphasis he placed upon instruction in theology. There was a historic confession that was part of the heritage of the church—that confession, the Apostles' Creed, constituted the outline of Calvin's first draft of the Institutes and of his catechism. Whether or not the

Apostles' Creed was actually formalized by the Apostles was uncertain, said Calvin, but the substance of it came from their teachings and probably was commonly declared by them.

Systematic theology comes into existence as a result of man's examination of the contents of Scripture and the organization of its doctrines in a logical form. Systematic theology enables man better to understand God, the works of God, the nature of man, the meaning of salvation, and the meaning of life. It was important to have intellectual knowledge of God and of God's purposes for his people.

Calvin was concerned about the unity of the church and believed that it would result from unity of doctrinal belief. He thought that the teachings of the Bible would commend themselves to theologians, and that the church would be led into a unity of fellowship. Calvin devoutly desired such fellowship in the church. However, while believing that unity in the church would result from unity in doctrinal belief, Calvin left little room for unity except on the theological bases he believed and taught. This was especially true of the views he entertained concerning the sacrament of the Lord's Supper. Luther, Calvin, and Zwingli held different views concerning the meaning of the Lord's Supper. When Calvin realized that those views could not be harmonized, he hoped that the various churches of the Reformation might still be united in a Federation, thus giving strength to the movement.

It is interesting to observe that Calvin used the Institutes in instructing pastors, theologians, and ministers, as well as adults. The Institutes had been prepared as a theological interpretation and exposition of the Scriptures, natural revelation, and God's activities in history, and were organized on the basis of the Apostles' Creed, the Ten Commandments, the Sacraments, and the Lord's Prayer.

Through theological instruction believers were to be solidly grounded in their faith. There would be a clear understanding of the differences between the doctrinal beliefs taught by the Reformers and the doctrines taught by the historic Roman Church. Men would be enabled to find answers to many of their questions. In dedicating the Institutes to "Francis, Most Christian King of the

French," Calvin wanted the king to know what the Reformation was teaching, what the Reformers believed. He wanted misunderstanding and erroneous charges made by enemies of the Reformation to be corrected and if possible dispelled. Thus, through the Institutes, the doctrines of the Christian faith, interpreted by the historic church, were taught by the Reformers for the edification of Christians.

Calvin believed that a much more simple instrument than the Institutes was needed for the instruction and indoctrination of children and young people. He therefore drafted a catechism as an instrument for their instruction. He wrote, "It has ever been the practice of the Church, and one carefully attended to, to see that children should be duly instructed in the Christian religion."[12] In order to provide for such instruction, schools were opened. Individuals were instructed in the contents of the catechism and how the catechism was to be taught. Pastors were the first teachers of the catechism, and it was customary for children to be publicly examined before the congregation on their knowledge of its contents. Such examinations were intended to show the faithfulness of parents in the instruction of their children. If children and young people were deficient in knowledge, their parents bore responsibility for it. Instruction in the catechism was basic for church membership. Baptized children were to be instructed thoroughly in the beliefs of the church, else they could not become communing members of the congregation. In offering catechetical instruction Calvin sought to revive a custom which the church had disregarded.

Calvin's catechism consisted of five sections: Of Faith, Of the Law (the Ten Commandments), Of Prayer, Of the Word of God, and Of the Sacraments. It is noteworthy that in his catechism Calvin left out any reference to the doctrine of predestination. He did this because he thought the doctrine, unless thoroughly understood, would cause people to stumble. He recognized how difficult it would be for older children and even young people to grasp this doctrine. Calvin's judgment in this matter still prevails among most educators and parents.

Two or three observations concerning Christian education as

practiced by Calvin may be pertinent. The first emphasis in instruction was placed upon a sound understanding and interpretation of the Bible. Adults were to be instructed in the Bible and in theology. Adults were then expected to teach the children and youth of the congregation, beginning in the home. Theological instruction was emphasized. The church was taught the message of the believing community. Special educational materials, in the form of the Institutes, catechism, and tracts, were used, and church history was taught. Commentaries were, in a sense, curriculum materials to be used in learning, teaching, and preaching. Educational materials had a definite place in the teaching ministry of the church.

Calvin placed great emphasis upon the importance of parental instruction in the home. This emphasis is reflected in the vows parents were required to take when they presented their children for the covenant of baptism. In the "Form of Administering Baptism," Calvin sets forth very clearly the biblical concept that children are members of the household of faith, and are to be beneficiaries of the covenant of grace. He writes: "There is no doubt that our children are heirs of the life which he has promised to us."[13] Calvin cites the instance of Jesus receiving children, and continues: "By declaring that the kingdom of heaven belongs to them, laying hands on them, and recommending them to God his Father, he clearly teaches that we must not exclude them from his Church. Following this rule then, we will receive this child into his Church."[14]

The following promise was to be made by parents who presented their children for baptism:

"As the object is to receive this child into the fellowship of the Christian Church, you promise, when it shall come to the years of discretion, to instruct it in the doctrine which is received by the people of God, as it is summarily comprehended in the Confession of Faith, which we all have, viz. . . . ."[15]

Following the parents' recitation of the Apostles' Creed, the vow continued: "You promise then to be careful to instruct it in all this doctrine, and generally in all that is contained in the Holy Scriptures . . . Likewise you will exhort it to live according to the rule which our Lord has laid down in his law, which is contained summarily in two points—to love God with all our heart and mind and strength, and our neighbour as ourselves: in like manner, to live according to the admonitions which God has given by his prophets and apostles, in order that renouncing itself and its own lusts, it may dedicate and consecrate itself to glorify the name of God and Jesus Christ, and edify its neighbour."[16]

These duties were kept constantly before parents, both by exhortation from the pulpit and by the yearly visitation of the pastors and elders in the homes of the people to inquire concerning their diligence in instructing their children.

In his writings Calvin expresses this devotional thought: "And if thou do me the worship to be a father, let me so bring up the children that thou shalt give me, as they may be rightly thine, so as they may learn to serve thee, and thou guide them according to thy good will."[17] He continues: "Such as have charge of others must be watchful. . . . Although I exhort . . . my children . . . to serve God; yet it is impossible for me to do all that I ought to do, for I see my children offend . . . Of whom take they it? Although I take pains to instruct them, yet are there many things to be found fault with, for I have not given them such example as I ought. Had I walked in the fear of God as becomes me, they must needs have followed my steps."[18] "They whom God has so far honoured as to give them children, let them consider that they are so much more bound to God to take pains that their children be well brought up. And if they will have been brought up well, they must always begin with religion. For children may in show have all the virtues in the world, but that is nothing unless they fear God and honour him. As we see a number that will take great pains to bring up their children in the affairs of this world . . . but to know God, there is no talk, no news of that. But this is not the way, this is to set the cart before the horse. Therefore . . . begin at this end to instruct children. For if they love God, it is a good foundation to build upon; but without it, there is nothing but ruin and confusion."[19]

Calvin, in stressing the necessity for parental correction and discipline of children, said, ". . . for what are my father and mother but the hands of God . . . ?"[20] He referred also to the unwillingness of young people to accept the counsel of their parents, believing themselves to be wise and full of knowledge. "Nowadays the world is so far out of order that young folks have gathered such in devilish pride as they be past receiving any manner of nurture or instruction at all, such of them as have any fear of God ought to fight so much the more against themselves, to the end they be not carried away after the common fashion."[21]

Then this very interesting comment is made: ". . . but . . . when old men discharge not their duty, young men may supply the room in that behalf, yea, even to the shame of those that have lived long, and misspent the time that God has given them, or rather utterly lost it. You see then . . . that the reverence which young folk bear to their elders . . . must not hinder the continual maintenance of the truth."[22] Calvin was zealous that God should be honored and vices suppressed even if the young had to take the lead.

Family religion was to reflect the offering of prayers before meals, after meals, early in the morning, and before retiring at night. The conduct of parents was recognized as being determinative in the religious faith and nurture of their children.

Some of the important elements in Christian nurture, as advocated and practiced by Calvin, clearly come to light. Children were to be presented to God in the covenant of baptism. They were to be instructed by their parents and in the church in the Word of God and the catechism. They were to be examined by pastors and elders in the presence of the members of the congregation. Children were to be properly guided and disciplined in the home. Youth were expected to show proper respect for the authority of parents. At the same time it was recognized that youth may have insights and views more truly consistent with the gospel than their parents manifest. Parents were urged to live godly lives before their children. These concepts, old as they may be, are understood by those engaged in Christian education today.

Christian Faith and Christian Ethics

Instruction in Christian faith and doctrine was vitally related to Christian ethics. One of the ways man glorifies God is by relating his faith to life so that it results in Christian conduct. Of the Reformers of the sixteenth and seventeenth centuries not one was more passionate in his conviction that Christian conduct was one of the essential marks of the Reformation than was John Calvin. He endeavored to control the behavior of men by the use of church discipline and civil law. He believed the preaching and teaching of the gospel would bear the fruit of Christian virtues and Christlike conduct. He instructed believers in the nature of Christian morals and ethics.

The relationship of the gospel to life, as understood by Calvin, is indicated in Chapter VII of Book III of the Institutes. In a forceful, convincing discussion, Calvin expounds the nature of the believer's life. It is a life that results from the believer's relationship with Christ. It grows out of the new life born of the Holy Spirit. It is the dedication of life to Christ by the believer in order that he may live to honor and glorify God daily. "It is the duty of believers to 'present their bodies a living sacrifice, holy, acceptable unto God.' "[23]

Calvin believed the church should describe the manner of conduct to be practiced by citizens of the community. He did not teach that the church was the state, as did Rome at that time. Nor did he believe, as did Luther, that the state should be freed from the rule of the church. He taught that the church and state were to be separate in certain areas of life and responsibility. The church was to have complete control over her own life, her statement of creeds and doctrines, and the administration of discipline. The state, on the other hand, was to administer civil laws. In the church-state relationship in Geneva, the church was to describe the laws of moral conduct which the City Council was to accept and enforce. This brought about tension and conflict in the city. Many Genevese were not members of the church. They regarded it as unreasonable that they should be compelled to live under the rigid moral laws the church taught. This basic difference between the Libertines and Calvin continued through all the years of Calvin's life in Geneva.

Previously, reference has been made to the conduct of citizens in Geneva in the sixteenth century. Historians write that there was much drunkenness, adultery, lewd behavior in taverns, profanity, stealing, and injustice among the citizens of the city. To permit such conduct to continue was not only to tolerate behavior the Ten Commandments forbade, Calvin declared, but as long as such conditions existed they brought temptation and corruption to others. Calvin wanted the laws to be rigidly enforced. Indeed, citizens were encouraged to report on the conduct of fellow citizens whom they knew or suspected to be guilty of improper conduct. Someone wrote that Calvin possessed both a "telescope and microscope" to search out the wicked!

The concept of the manner in which the state was expected to enforce the laws of conduct determined by the church is subject to debate. What is not subject to debate is that Calvin believed the preaching and teaching of the gospel to be relevant to life. Conduct becoming Christians was a matter of concern to the church. Parents were expected to teach their children that the gospel makes demands upon them. Officers and pastors were to administer discipline and to exercise control over all members of the church. Discipline was designed to be redemptive, but if the offender did not repent and reform he was excommunicated. The state was to control and discipline the lives of her citizens. A. M. Hunter aptly states the contrast between Luther's view and that of Calvin as follows: "For Luther the Church was the keeper of the State's conscience; for Calvin, it was the instructor and regulator of that conscience."[24] He continues: "While the civil power had no right to make laws concerning religion and divine worship, it must keep the Church purged of offences by punishment or coercion. It is the business of the State 'to foster and maintain the external worship of God, to defend sound doctrine and the condition of the church, . . . to see that no blasphemy against the name of God, no calumnies against His truth nor other offences against religion, break out and be disseminated amongst the people; . . . in short, that a public form of religion may exist among Christians and humanity among men.' "[25]

The reform of life was a matter of concern to Calvin. He knew that evil conduct existed in the church. The immorality of certain priests, bishops, and popes is a matter of record. Such conduct is unworthy of those who belong to the visible church. The state was expected to be the arm of the church in controlling the conduct of all citizens. One of the customs of the church that contributed to immorality was the sale of indulgences. In the dedication of his Institutes to Francis I, Calvin described plainly the depravity and greed of the church leaders. "Indeed," said Calvin, "they universally exert themselves for the preservation of their kingdom, and the repletion of their bellies; but not one of them discovers [reveals] the least indication of sincere zeal."[26]

The Character of the Teacher and Preacher

Those who taught or preached were expected to live exemplary lives. In a letter Calvin addressed to ministers he reminded them that people boast of a knowledge of the Bible and yet often live licentious lives, as if the gospel were not a rule of life. He reminded them that when the Jews called God their legislator and then failed to live by his laws, God was justly displeased with them. It was regarded as equally reprehensible for teachers and preachers of the gospel to express great concern for the doctrine of Christ while at the same time trampling its teachings under foot by their headstrong and libidinous course of life, thereby dishonoring the Master by their transgressions.

Teachers of the gospel were urged to reflect prudence and skill in giving advice. Such traits of character reflect wisdom. Harshness of spirit or speech would deprive instruction of its use and value.

Regarding teaching, Calvin observed that when one presumes to teach others he must examine himself to see that he bears the image of Christ in his own life. Then one could truly teach the things he believes in and practices, thereby convincing others that he speaks from his heart, and that he does not tell a tale as a player might play his part in a drama.

It is impossible for the preacher and teacher of the gospel to separate his teaching from his life. The life of the preacher is a witness to the truth and power of the gospel he proclaims. To disregard this would mean that his words were like "sounding brass, or a tinkling cymbal."[27]

Concern for the Poor

The physical condition of the citizens of Geneva was a matter of deep concern to Calvin. The sick and homeless were to receive the pastoral care of the minister. Calvin knew the meaning of poverty. He never received a munificent salary, and often he was in dire want. In Strasbourg he suffered deep hunger because of his lack of money to buy food. He probably jeopardized his life at that time, for he never seemed to regain the physical strength he formerly had possessed. He suffered weakness the remaining years of his life. In Geneva, due to sickness, Calvin was reduced to a mere subsistence. At his death he left an inheritance which could not have been valued at more than a thousand dollars. During his life, he gave of his meager funds to minister to the poor. When the Black Plague swept over the city he insisted on going to live among those who suffered illness. The unfortunate sick had little hope of recovery from the deadly plague, and Calvin knew they should have pastoral care. He offered himself for this ministry, but the City Council refused to let him perform such a service, knowing how important it was for him to be spared to carry on the work he had begun. During his lifetime Calvin opened his home to many destitute people and gave of his limited resources to relieve the wretched condition of the poor. In his will, Calvin left ten guineas to be given to relieve the destitute in the city.

Anyone seeking an understanding of the nature of the "pure gospel" soon learns, from Calvin's life and works, that the term means infinitely more than a message of divine truth. The gospel is the good news of God's redeeming grace. It calls for a way of life that reflects the love and righteousness of God, and the state as well as the church rests under God's judgment. Calvin took seriously the teachings and ministry of Jesus concerning the poor. Social service was not left to forces or agencies outside the church. Such service was to be an expression of the faith and love of those who belonged to the church.

Calvin understood the needs of the Reformation as well as any man of his day. He knew that the essential message of the gospel is contained in the Old and New Testaments. He believed that the heart of the doctrines of the Bible is to be found in the words of the Apostles' Creed. The doctrines of the Scriptures had been twisted, distorted, and misrepresented for centuries. For the authority of Scripture in matters of faith and life, man had substituted the authority of tradition and the church. Errors of belief were accompanied by errors of government and discipline. Such conditions called for a complete break with the church that would not consider reform from within. Calvin attacked the errors of the church not piecemeal but in entirety. Félix Bungener wrote of Calvin: "Calvin the Reformer had long understood that the Reformation must live and grow by knowledge, and called upon all its partisans to exercise really and sincerely the right which it conferred upon them of knowing for and by themselves the things of faith. . . . In a short time it had everywhere prepared learned, able, and ardent champions, who were in their turn to prepare others."[28]

Calvin's Emphasis Upon Education

Calvin knew the Reformation would be weak as long as the citizens of Geneva lacked the education they needed to understand and advance the message of the Word of God. He advocated the establishment of schools in the city. It was many years after the request was made of the Council before it finally authorized the establishment of a college. The college was planned by Calvin. True, there had been prior to that time some early efforts by William Farel to establish schools in Geneva, but the effort failed for a lack of thorough planning. In 1559 the College of Geneva was constituted. On June 25, city officials went to St. Peter's where the ministers of the Word of God and the learned doctors were gathered. There in the Cathedral, Calvin offered a prayer in which he gave thanks to God for the college that was to be constituted, and invoked the blessings of God upon it. The Council's formal statement that authorized the building of the college was read. The form of confession to be made by the faculty and rector was cited. There would be five members of the faculty: two would teach theology, one Hebrew, one Greek, and one philosophy. Provisions for teaching medicine and law would come later.

The school held a prominent place in the affections of the people of Geneva. Except for the Cathedral, no building was dearer to their hearts. Many of Calvin's writings, letters, and works were kept in it. The durability and permanence of the Reformation in Geneva can be attributed in part to the Academy. Citizens of Geneva were disciplined through education as well as theology.

The last years of Calvin's life were free from some of the bitter struggles he had waged earlier. While opposition to his rigid concepts of life never died out, the citizens of Geneva, and particularly the city fathers, recognized the utter sincerity of their pastor and knew from bitter experience that unrighteousness breeds crime, division, and misery.

Calvin coveted no honor in life or in death. He directed that there should be no memorial service and no eulogy at his death. He wanted his body buried without ceremony and left to rest in a spot unmarked by monument or stone. This was done. Inscribed on the register of the city of Geneva is this entry, "Went to God, Saturday the 27th."

Calvin's name is perpetuated in history. His influence on theological thought, education, government, economics, and ethics has been notable in practically every Western nation. Through Presbyterian churches established on every continent, his influence on the visible church is still profound. Rénan said of Calvin: "He succeeded because he was the most Christian man of the century."

There are views and positions in Calvin's theology as expressed in his commentaries which are not readily accepted by many trustworthy theologians today. He wrote before the teachings of Copernicus were widely known, and his views of the universe and science are not wholly accurate. He taught a view of the doctrine of predestination and reprobation which appears to some not to take into account the emphasis the gospel places upon the activities of God in history, upon God's love, and upon God's call to all men to believe. It is difficult to account fully for man's freedom and responsibility for his transgressions in the forceful, clear logic of Calvin's interpretation of the Bible. Calvin's teachings are criticized, also, because they do not reflect any great missionary concern for the nations of the world. Wesley regarded Calvin's teaching as "monstrous." He has been accused of teaching fatalism and of being a moral dictator.

Yet, there are tangible evidences of the strength and greatness of his life and work. Calvin's writings include the *Institutes of the Christian Religion,* commentaries on the Bible, over two thousand sermons, and numerous tracts and letters. He taught the dignity of human nature and the responsibility of the community to its citizens. He was both democratic and socialistic in his views of man. His teachings magnify the worth of the daily labors of every man. The American Revolution and the concept of representative government had their origin in the teachings of John Calvin.

A. M. Hunter has written appropriately as follows: "Calvinism is, of course, primarily the teaching of Calvin in its widest scope. . . . Piety was the keynote of his character. He was a God-possessed man. . . . Calvin's doctrine of predestination might well have issued in a fatalism which induced a paralysis of ethical endeavour. It actually did the very reverse. It braced men's wills. . . . It inspired them to a strenuous and heroic activity which brought about a very miracle of moral revolution in all spheres of life and all quarters of the world. So much more was it the spirit of Calvinism which counted than its letter. . . . Everywhere it awakened and made sensitive lethargic consciences. It created a refined, if vehement, piety which blossomed into a strength and frequent beauty of high character that has since been the world's most valuable asset. Calvin's religion was reflected in his crest—a hand with a burning heart in it, and the words, 'I give Thee all.' That is what it meant to him, and what it meant to him he taught to others. Calvinism in a word stood for consecration, the consecration that found its ideal and example in the Christ whose tired feet climbed Mount Olivet to pray and the hill Calvary to die."[29] Calvin was the very incarnation of one who reflected "humble dependence upon God, of patient submission to His holy will, of whole-hearted consecration to His service, of perfect trust in His sleepless care and unchanging love. . . . Where men with a high gravity live life under a profound sense of responsibility and a keen realisation of its incalculable issues in eternity, where a community, a society, a people bow to the imperious claims of a Christianised conscience and seek to order their affairs under its direction, there Calvinism lives."[30]

Calvin's concepts of Christian nurture were valid in his day and are valid today.

3 | JOHN KNOX
AND CHRISTIAN EDUCATION

"With the single exception of the period which covers the intro-
duction and first marvellous triumphs of Christianity, the Reformation of the sixteenth century must be owned as perhaps the
greatest and most glorious revolution in the history of the human
race,"[1] wrote Alexander F. Mitchell.

Origins of the Reformation in Scotland

The Reformation in Scotland had its origin in many sources. It
developed because of conditions in that country, because of the
moral predicament of man, because of corruption in the church,
because of corruption in government, and because of the rebirth of
faith resulting from the reading and understanding of the Scriptures.

There was widespread ignorance and corruption of life among
the people of Scotland, as in the rest of Europe, during the thirteenth, fourteenth, and fifteenth centuries. Many of the priests
were illiterate. They were not versed in the Scriptures nor trained
to engage in original study. They were taught to accept the interpretations and declarations of church officials. Being unenlightened
in biblical content and exegesis they were unable to enlighten
others. The masses of the people also were illiterate. Had the
Bible been translated into the vernacular, they still would have
been unable to read it. Ignorance leads to corruption, and it did in
Scotland.

The church was corrupt morally and spiritually. Churchmen in high places were notoriously profligate. Immorality was practiced and condoned at every level of church position. Local priests, as well as bishops, archbishops, and in some instances popes, kept their mistresses and concubines. Bastard children of church officials were given benefices that resulted in munificent financial returns. Often, the illegitimate children of church officials were given seats of honor at formal dinners and banquets. The brazen conduct of such leaders insulted the standards of honor and morality yet lingering in the hearts and minds of the people. Conditions cried out for reform.

The church had grown rich and fat with wealth gained at the expense of the poor. Peasants were brought down to poverty by their lords who, in turn, were compelled to give liberal financial support to the church. More than one third of the land and wealth of Scotland at that time was owned by the church. In addition to the demands made upon the peasants by their lords, money was extracted from them by the church through the sale of indulgences. And, as if this were not too much, priests and bishops demanded costly payment for the baptism of children, the performance of the marriage ceremony, and the burial of the dead. Without such payment, these functions were not performed.

The church possessed great power and grew arrogant in the use of it. The crimes and sins of dukes and heads of clans in Scotland could be pardoned by their archbishops, who were granted this power by Rome. Of course the dukes and clan leaders were compelled to pay handsomely for such favors. This cost, also, was exacted of the miserable peasants. The lords of the land resisted the power of the Crown and sought alliance with the church to escape domination by their civil rulers. The success of Henry VIII of England in wresting power from the church brought fear to the Romanists in Scotland. They sought help from France to retain their royal privileges. Little, if any, moral or spiritual power remained in the church, and there were no evidences that its leaders desired to bring about a reformation.

The people were desperately poor. They were underpaid, underfed, and abused. They could be arrested for the slightest supposed wrong, jailed for nonpayment of debts, or driven from their homes for their failure to make enough from the sale of their crops to pay their landlords. They were unable to secure help when there was sickness in the home.

Ignorant and unlettered as the people of Scotland were, there was within them an innate sense of decency. They were troubled in conscience at what they saw happening in the name of religion. The sight of corruption and immoral conduct did not harmonize with the people's understanding of the nature of God. "Yet," wrote Dr. Alexander Mitchell, "it must never be forgotten that, even in these degenerate days, there were those among the ministers of the church who wept in secret over the abominations that were done, who longed for the dawn of a better day, and . . . sought to prepare the way for it."[2]

The church was as corrupt in doctrinal beliefs and teachings as it was in life and conduct. What the church taught about the forgiveness of sins was false; sin cannot be atoned through the payment of wealth. What the church failed to teach about righteousness was tragic. Neither state nor church hierarchy is free from the demands of the law of God. All people are subject to his judgment. The doctrine of the infallibility of religious leaders was false, as was the declaration that the decrees of church councils are more authoritative than the Scriptures.

During this period an occasional scholar would find the truth God has made known to man in the written revelation, the Bible. The diligent, scholarly study of the Scripture by such men as Wycliffe, Tyndale, Coverdale, Luther, and Calvin brought the hidden light of God's Word to bear upon the darkened minds and hearts of men. The message of grace was heard. The call to men to put their faith in Christ and in him alone for salvation brought hope and joy to those who lived in despair. Clearly, the Word of God called men to a life of righteousness and love. The Protestant Reformation was born out of a discovery of the message of the gospel, found in the Word of God. It was in the context of such an age that John Knox lived and led the forces of the Reformation in Scotland.

A Brief Word About John Knox

John Knox was born in the early part of the sixteenth century. One historian gives the date of Knox's birth as 1505. Theodore Beza placed the date as late as 1515. James McEwen states that Knox was born in 1514, the year indicated by recent research. It is known that Knox was born in the fertile farming section of Scotland, in East Lothian, near the town of Haddington. His peasant parents were subjects of Lord Bothwell. His father was William Knox. His mother was a Sinclair. He was educated in Haddington and probably at the University of St. Andrews. Knox evidently taught school in Haddington for about twenty years. By 1543 he was known as a priest in his native town. He was called "Sir John Knox," the usual designation of a priest who had not obtained a Master's degree.

George Wishart, a fiery preacher of the Reformation, made a great impression on Knox. When Wishart was about to be arrested for his activities and preaching, Knox planned to defend him even though Lord Bothwell had ordered the arrest. Wishart would not permit Knox to remain with him, saying, "One is sufficient for a sacrifice."[3]

Cardinal Beaton of St. Andrews was responsible for the death of George Wishart in 1546. Knox was in the diocese of St. Andrews when certain men who belonged to the Reform movement conspired to assassinate the Cardinal because of his insistence upon the death of a leader of this Reformation. While Knox denounced the action of the Cardinal in killing Wishart, he could not condone the action of the Cardinal's murderers. In strong language Knox denounced also that bloody deed. The moral courage of the man and the fiery eloquence he displayed prompted the men of the castle and town to approach Knox and request him to become chaplain and minister at the castle. Although such a call to the ministry was not of Knox's desire or plans, he was unable to resist the invitation extended to him. As a result of this call, Knox entered upon the pulpit work that was to distinguish his ministry for the remainder of his life.

Knox's services in St. Andrews were marked also by his teach-

ing. He offered instruction in the Gospel According to John. Following the example of Wishart, he catechized his pupils on the
lessons they had studied.

To his preaching and teaching Knox added his attack upon the
customs of the church. He declared that all ceremonies devised
by man for the worship of God, without express warrant of Scripture, were idolatry. The central elements of the Reformation as
Knox viewed them were thus evident early in his ministry. They
were prophetic preaching, sound instruction, and the reform of
the church.

The events that took place in St. Andrews brought the forces
of France to the little university town. The city was sacked. Knox
was taken prisoner. He was made to serve on a galley ship as a
slave. For nineteen months his life was one of agony and torturous
labor. Knox's release from the galley ship was most likely secured
through the intervention of the young king of England, Edward
VI. This young king was not only friendly to the Reformation but
also gave active support to the work of the Reformers. He appointed Knox to preach in England. Knox preached in the border
town of Keswick. It was while he was in Keswick that he became
engaged to Marjorie Bowes, one of fifteen children of Richard
and Elizabeth Bowes. The friendship of Knox and Elizabeth
Bowes, his genuine pastoral concern for a woman who was undoubtedly earnest in her desire to be instructed in the faith of the
Reformers, is one of the intensely interesting complications of
Knox's life.

Upon the untimely death of Edward VI, Mary Tudor, known as
Bloody Mary, became Queen of England in 1553. Knox, at the
earnest request of his friends, fled to the continent. His stay in
Frankfurt as minister to English refugees was marked by conflict,
due to his refusal to use the English Prayer Book. Members of
the group finally voted him out of office, and in order to restore
peace to the church, he left the city.

Geneva was the next place Knox visited. He was drawn there
by the preaching and teaching of John Calvin. Under Calvin's
ministry Knox became thoroughly grounded in the doctrines of
the Reformation. He was greatly impressed by Calvin's leadership

in Geneva and called that city the most Christlike community he had ever seen. Knox's studies on the continent included Hebrew and Greek. With Calvin and Bullinger, Knox discussed the relationship of the civil authorities and the church. He posed the question, "Should the godly obey a magistrate who enforces idolatry and condemns true religion?" Among the views developed while Knox was on the continent was the conviction that solitary piety in a man's religious life was not enough. Reform had to include the reform of government and society.

Knox was deeply interested in developments taking place in Scotland. From the continent he wrote letters to the nobles of the land. Some of the cardinal ideas Knox advocated and developed are reflected in his letters. In a letter to the Queen Regent of Scotland he urged her to consent to the reading of the Bible in the language of the people and to embrace the evangelical faith. To the people of Scotland he wrote that they must hold fast to their views on the Reformation. He counseled parents to remember that they were as "bishops" in their home, and charged them with the responsibility of teaching their children the faith and belief to which they were giving their loyalties.

It was not until 1559 that Knox was permitted to return to Scotland for his significant work of reform. The years that followed, through 1566, were the most successful of his ministry. The Queen Regent promised religious reform, at Knox's insistence and threats and upon demands made by her nobles. Knox and five other men whose names began with "John" drew up the Confession of Faith and the Book of Discipline. These were adopted by the church, and the Confession was readily approved by Parliament. Knox wanted the lords of the Parliament to approve the Book of Discipline also, as he was intent upon bringing about reform in civil as well as church government. While most of the members of the Scottish Parliament subscribed to the instruments Knox and his associates had written, they did not officially ratify the Book of Discipline. But the force of the Reformation was in full sway. It looked as if the struggle for reform was won.

The history of Scotland is marked by plots, intrigue, and swift changes. In 1560 the Queen Dowager died, and the following summer Mary Stuart, Queen of the Scots, returned from France. The turbulent sessions between the charming young queen and John Knox highlight one of the dramatic periods of Scotland's history. The queen was a devout Roman Catholic, determined to bring Scotland back to the faith of Rome. She made every effort to restore the Roman Church in Scotland, and Knox was the one person who consistently and courageously opposed her. Uncompromising at all times, rude some of the time, bold and fearless always, Knox withstood the charms and tears of the queen, exposed and resisted the nobles who supported her, led the struggle that the Reformers had begun, awakened courage in them when they became faint of heart, and brought the Reformation movement to a triumphant establishment in the land.

Mary hastened her own downfall. The marriage to Lord Darnley resulted in failure. The Italian prince and counselor, Rizzio, was murdered with the aid of Darnley, who himself was murdered a few months later. Early courtship and marriage between Mary and Bothwell were too much even for the people who really wanted a queen. The fury of the people brought about Mary's imprisonment. She escaped and sought refuge in England, where after years of further imprisonment she was beheaded in 1587 by order of her kinswoman Elizabeth.

Knox's last days were neither brilliant nor happy. His first wife died. A few years later he was married again, and to a very young woman. He had made himself obnoxious to certain nobles of the land by his bold, ruthless attacks upon the queen. Although Knox maintained a strong influence over the continuing Reformation, he did not again reach the height of influence he had enjoyed in the early 1560's. He returned to the pulpit in St. Andrews where he had first preached as a minister. Much of the burning fire of the man was in his heart and voice. "He banged his fist so hard the pulpit was like to break into splinters," wrote one of his friends.

Knox died in 1572. He was buried just outside the walls of St. Giles Church. The Regent Morton, as he stood by the grave, said, "Here lies one who neither flattered nor feared any flesh."[4]

In the works and writings of Knox there are reflected some significant concepts of Christian education. These point to basic views found in the history of the Presbyterian and Reformed Churches of the world.

The Understanding and Use of the Bible

The authority of the Bible is of central importance in Christian education, as it is in preaching. Knox's understanding of the Bible and the influence the Bible had upon his life and ministry are reflected in almost every letter he wrote, whether to the lords of Scotland, to the Queen Regent, to the "Monstruous Woman," or to friends. James Stalker wrote: "The weapon with which Knox fought this battle was the Word of God."[5] The Bible was the book Knox studied most, and his reading was done in a spirit of genuine devotion. As he familiarized himself with the content of the Bible, he memorized it and let its message possess him thoroughly. What he learned from his study caused him to break with Romanism. The Bible was of course the basis of his preaching and gave him the necessary courage and inspiration for his leadership of the Reformation. The man who did so much to bring the new light of the Reformation to Scotland, who preached with such moving power, and who aroused a populace that was hopelessly disgusted with what it beheld in the church and nation, was a master of the Bible and was mastered by it. He who was to teach and instruct others was himself instructed by the Book he loved and studied.

Knox's personal love of the Scriptures is reflected in this statement from his pen: "I delight in nothing so much as in the simple and native meaning of the Scriptures, as they be alleged in their own places by the Holy Ghost."[6] He had a particular love for the Old Testament. This is indicated by his frequent quotations from it. His interpretations occasionally reflect an exegesis present-day biblical scholars would not sanction, but Knox found analogies in the Bible that served his purposes well. Perhaps it was Knox's love for the Old Testament and intensive study of it that kept him from reflecting upon and emphasizing the message of grace, forgiveness, and redemption set forth in the Gospels and the Epistles. But no one can doubt Knox's belief in the sufficiency of the Scriptures and in their authority in all matters pertaining to the faith and life of the church. In Knox's *History of the Reformation in Scotland* he writes: "As we believe and confess the Scriptures of God sufficient to instruct and make the man of God perfect, so do we affirm and avow the authority of the same to be of God, and neither to depend on men nor angels. We affirm therefore that such as allege the Scripture to have no [other] authority, but that which is received from the Kirk, to be blasphemous against God, and injurious to the true Kirk, which always heareth and obeyeth the voice of her own Spouse and Pastor, but taketh not upon her to be mistress over the same."[7] This view was in marked contrast to the view of the Roman Church of that period. Knox believed the Scriptures were authenticated by God, not by the word of the church. The "Kirk" was under the authority of the Scriptures and derived its understanding of the will of God from the Scriptures as they were illumined by the Holy Spirit.

Knox's concept of the authority of the Scriptures is important. Completely loyal to the Bible as the inspired account of God's revelation to man, he repeatedly emphasized the belief that the authority of the Scriptures is based upon the fact that God speaks in them and through them. God authenticates the Word. Nowhere in the writings of Knox has there been found any indication that he believed the authority of the Scriptures to be based upon a specific theory concerning the manner in which they were inspired. One position frequently reflected in his writings was the belief that the Word of God could be understood, preached, and taught only through the illumination and work of the Holy Spirit.

To be a preacher was to Knox the highest office in the church. "I am called," he told Queen Mary, "to a public function within the Church of God, and am appointed by God to rebuke the sins and vices of all."[8] He felt obliged to cry out—to be a trumpet. "I am not master of myself," he told Queen Mary again, "but must obey him who commands me to speak plain and to flatter no flesh upon the face of the earth."[9] He sternly warned of the judgment of God. He prophesied judgment for the sins of corruption and for religious forms of worship contrary to the Word of God. In the activities of God in Bible history, Knox saw how God was acting in the history of his own day. The Bible was, to him, a living Book.

The Use of the Bible by the People

It is doubtful if there was any nation in the mid-sixteenth century which was more concerned about the use of the Bible by the people than was Scotland, as reflected in the work of its Reformers. They wanted the Bible to be in the hands of the people. Even before Knox's leadership was clearly established, the spirit of the Reformation prompted the nobles to join the struggling Reformers in petitioning and securing from the Crown the right to read the Bible in the vernacular. They gained permission to have the services of the church in the language the people could understand. Knox, in his eagerness that the people should read the Bible, made the reading of the Bible one of the central elements of the Reformation in Scotland.

In the fifteen hundred years of the history of the Christian Church the use of the Bible had undergone several changes. During the first four centuries, the Bible, written on scrolls, was read by members of the Christian fellowship with the encouragement of their leaders. Chrysostom urged laymen not to leave it to the clergy to interpret the Bible but to interpret it for themselves. The barbarians overran Rome and the entire empire in the fifth and sixth centuries. Education received mortal injury. The Dark Ages followed. The laity were unable to read. The interpretation of the Bible was in the hands of an increasingly smaller number of priests. By the time education was revived and some of the laity at least were able to read, the church discouraged the reading of the Bible by the laity. "Before the middle of the thirteenth century the councils of Toulouse and Tarragona 'forbade the laity to read the vernacular translations of the Bible.' "[10] The opposition continued and increased. "In the second half of the sixteenth century, 'Pius IV. required the bishops to refuse lay persons leave to read even Catholic versions of Scripture unless their confessors or parish priests judged that such reading was likely to prove beneficial.' "[11] In spite of this, there were occasional groups of people who did read the Scriptures. Among them were the Waldensians of northern Italy and the Hussites of Bohemia. Such reading of the Scriptures invariably resulted in a new life of faith and conduct in the people. Methods of Bible study in those days included typology and allegory, considered to be keys to the unlocking of biblical truth. Faith meant, primarily, assent to a creed formulated by the church. Browning wrote an interesting "Soliloquy of the Spanish Cloister" and its interpretation of the Bible:

> "There's a great text in Galatians,
>   Once you trip on it, entails
> Twenty-nine distinct damnations,
>   One sure, if another fails."[12]

Such views, typical of the church of the fifteenth and sixteenth centuries, made the revolutionary positions of Knox appear bold beyond belief.

Knox's view of the Bible is set forth in his first interview with Mary Queen of Scots. He told the queen, "The word of God is plain in the self; and if there appear any obscurity in one place, the Holy Ghost, which is never contrarious to himself, explains the same more clearly in other places: so that there can remain no doubt but unto such as obstinately remain ignorant."[13]

Emphasis was placed upon the lucidity and unity of the Scriptures, and upon the necessity of interpreting Scripture in the light of Scripture to safeguard against the apparent meaning of an isolated passage taken out of context.

While Knox was on the continent he addressed a letter to the lairds of Scotland in 1556. He offered counsel to the Reformers and the church. His advice is contained in the following lengthy quotation from his letter:

"Considering that St. Paul calleth the congregation 'the body of Christ,' whereof every one of us is a member, teaching us thereby that no member is of sufficiency to sustain and feed itself without the help and support of another, I think it necessary, for the conference of Scriptures, assemblies of brethren to be had. The order therein to be observed is expressed by St. Paul, and therefore need not I to use many words in that behalf; only expressing my wish, that, when ye convene or come together—which I would were once a week—that your beginning should be from confession of your offences and invocation of the Spirit of the Lord Jesus to assist you in all your godly enterprises. And then let some place of Scripture be plainly and distinctly read, so much as shall be thought sufficient for one day or time; which ended, if any brother have exhortation, question or doubt, let him not fear to speak or move the same, so that he do it with moderation, either to edify or to be edified. And hereof I doubt not great profit shall shortly ensue; for, first, by hearing, reading and conferring the Scriptures in the assembly, the whole body of the Scriptures of God shall become familiar, the judgments and spirits of men shall be tried, their patience and modesty shall be known, and, finally, their gifts and utterance shall appear."[14] Here was Bible study. Groups of people met together to read and comment upon the Scriptures. Readers were encouraged to ask questions. If there were any doubts, those doubts were to be disclosed. The chances were that someone in the group could help shed light upon a biblical passage and that doubts could be resolved thereby. Each learned from all the others. Such group Bible study was strongly advocated by Knox.

Another interesting word of counsel to readers of the Bible was that they were to read the Bible in sections or large blocks of content. They were warned against reading "snippets" of the Bible and thinking that such reading would be of the most help in understanding the Scriptures.

Knox's advice to the church continues: "If anything occur within the text, or else arise in reasoning, which your judgments cannot resolve or your capacities apprehend, let the same be noted and put in writing, before ye dismiss the congregation, that, when God shall offer unto you any interpreter, your doubts, being noted and known, may have the more expedient resolution . . . Of myself I will speak as I think: I will more gladly spend fifteen hours in communicating my judgment with you, in explaining as God pleases to open to me any place of Scripture, than half an hour in any other matter."[15] Knox recognized the value of using persons who had some competence in interpreting the Scriptures to meet with groups who had raised questions they could not answer. He pointed out the joy and satisfaction he found in seeking light from the Scripture rather than from other sources, and then in speaking of the insights he had derived from the Word of God.

Another important principle of Bible study was advocated by Knox. He urged readers and students to study from the Old Testament and the New Testament until all the Bible was read. He knew that the Old Testament pointed to the New Testament, enfolding its promises and hopes. He believed that the New Testament shed light upon the Old Testament and contained the story of the fulfillment in Christ of the covenant promises.

The attitude of the persons engaged in reading and studying the Bible was a matter of great importance in the mind of Knox. He was concerned lest those who advanced their views or spoke in answer to questions should be argumentative and obstinate. Therefore he urged them to be content not to win an argument but to attempt to arrive at an understanding of truth. They were to seek the true message of the Scriptures, being guided, edified, and strengthened by what they would learn from them. Through prayer the guidance of the Holy Spirit was sought. Their sessions of study were to begin with prayer and close with prayer.

The radical nature of this departure from the customs of the Roman Church is evident. Here was a bold effort to put the Bible into the hands of the people. The people were expected to interpret, explain, and expound the Word of God. They were not to be dependent upon priests or ministers. Knox was confident that the basic message of the Word of God, the heart of any passage, could be easily discerned as men heard God speak in it and through it. This use of the Bible was one of the boldest changes advocated by the Reformers.

In other ages, particularly today, the Bible has been a closed book, not because men have been forbidden to read it but because they have neglected to read it. The Bible has not been understood because it has not been read properly. The living Word of God can fail as completely when it is unread, unstudied, and unbelieved, as it has failed when governments of state or church have legislated against the use of it or forbidden men to read it for themselves. There is a vital correlation between genuine Bible study and the Reformation. "Knox gave the Bible to Scotland, taught his countrymen to know and love it and to recognize in it that divine authority which is above all authorities on earth."[16]

Religious Instruction in the Home

Knox stressed religious instruction in the home. The service of baptism described in the Book of Discipline reminded parents of their obligation. They were directed to present their children for the covenant of baptism and were cautioned not to delay, as it was important that from the earliest days of the child's life he should be within the covenant and fellowship of the visible church. Baptism was to be administered by the minister. The service of baptism was not to be a private ceremony, but a family and congregational service of worship. At the time the child was presented for baptism the parents were required to renew their profession of faith in Christ, using the words of the Apostles' Creed. They then affirmed their intention of bringing the child up in the doctrines and beliefs of the church and of reading the Bible daily to the child.

Families were expected to read the Bible together each day and to memorize it. Parents, especially fathers, were directed to instruct their children in the faith of the church. One historian commented that by the time the church had adopted the Confession of Faith and the Book of Discipline there was a Bible in every home in Scotland, readily available and frequently used.

Knox advocated that children and youth be questioned regularly in church after their instruction in the home. "For, first," said he, "the youths and tender children shall be nourished and brought up in virtue, in presence of their friends . . . Secondarily, the exercise of the children in every church shall be great instruction to the aged."[17]

Knox prepared a catechism to be used in offering religious instruction to children and youth. He used it in his own teaching and directed the church, especially the minister of the church, to use it. The catechism was used particularly in the preparation of children for admission to Communion. This was regarded as the minister's first duty. Knox believed that at least two years of instruction were necessary to provide proper training for those who were to receive the sacrament of the Lord's Supper for the first time. Training children at home and reading the Bible to the family were like the practice of the Children of Israel in eating manna daily in the wilderness, thought Knox. So were the families of Scotland urged to feed upon the Word of God daily.

In the Genevan Church children were admitted to Communion when they were fifteen years of age. In France and Scotland they were expected to come to the Communion table at the age of twelve.

The Instruction of Youth

The First Book of Discipline, prepared by Knox and five of his colleagues, outlined a plan for the education of the youth of Scotland. The plan called for a series of schools in every "Toun." The schools were to be established and conducted by the church. Every boy and girl was to have at least four years of education. At the end of those four years the children who passed their examinations were to continue their studies for six additional years. As meager as four years of education may seem to one living in the twentieth century, such a program was a radical innovation in a period when illiteracy had flourished for centuries and even most of the leaders of the church were illiterate.

After the four and six year periods of instruction had been offered, Knox envisioned the establishment of universities providing instruction in theology, medicine, and law.

Knox's plan was a bold one. He advocated education that was to be permeated with religious instruction, a plan that would put God at the center of education.

There had to be some way to finance the system of schools Knox advocated. He believed this could be done by using a part of the confiscated holdings of the Roman Church. Provisions for carrying out Knox's scheme for education were contained in the First Book of Discipline, rejected by the Scottish Parliament. For a number of years prior to the Reformation, ecclesiastical property had been passing into the hands of the nobles, barons, and gentry, and the lords were unwilling to lose control of this source of revenue, which was often diverted into their own pockets.

Public school education for every child was conceived in the minds of the Reformers. Part of their concept of the Reformation was that the ability to read would enable the people to discover the meaning of God's Word for themselves, and that through education people would be prepared for useful, intelligent service to the church or the state. Youths were taught that at the age of twenty-four they were to be prepared to serve either the church or their nation through their daily vocation.

Knox's plan for religious instruction was presented in specific terms in the Book of Discipline. "In 'greit Tounis' there was to be a sermon or 'Commoun Prayeris' daily 'with some exercise of reiding the Scripturis;' and in each 'notable Toun' there was to be sermon and prayers on one day of the week besides Sunday. In every church there was to be a Bible 'in Inglesche,' which was to be read systematically to the congregation from beginning to end. Each head of a household was to be responsible for the religious knowledge both of his children and his servants. 'And gif thay stuburnlie continew, and suffer thair children and servandis to continew in wilfull ignorance, the discipline of the Churche must proceid against them unto excommunicatioun; and then must the mater be referred to the Civill Magistrat.' "[18]

Knox's plan was further outlined. "In every place, where men of fitting gifts were found, there was to be a weekly meeting for the discussion of such passages in Scripture as might tend to mutual edification. At these weekly 'prophesyings,' as they are termed, all were to be present to whom any talent had been committed for the spiritual profit of their fellows. 'And yf any be found disobedient,' is the solemn threat, 'and not willing to communicat the giftis and spirituall graces of God with thair brethren, after sufficient admonitioun, discipline must procead against thame; provided that the Civile Magistrate concur with the judgement and electioun of the Churche. For no man may be permitted to leave [live] as best pleasseth him within the Churche of God; but everie man must be constrayned by fraternall admonitioun and correctioun to bestow his laubouris when of the Churche thei ar required to the edificatioun of otheris."[19] Nothing like this was found in any country of Europe. "Through the various means of edification provided for him, every Scotsman was subjected to a moral and intellectual discipline such as no other country succeeded in giving to its people. To this discipline, far more than to the parish schools, has been due that

Stately speech;

Such as grave Livers do in Scotland use,
Religious men, who give to God and man their dues."[20]

Knox's Views on the Sacraments

The sacraments are a means of grace. They were instituted by Christ to proclaim the gospel. To imply that Knox viewed the sacraments as part of his concept of Christian nurture would give a twist to the views Knox held of them. At the same time, the way in which the sacrament of baptism was to be observed when parents presented their children for this sacrament definitely reveals and emphasizes the importance Knox attached to the covenant relationship between God and the parents of the child. The parents were reminded of their responsibility to teach the child the principles of the faith they professed.

The covenant of baptism was to be entered into between God and the parents, who were exercising faith on behalf of the child receiving the sacrament. It was not necessary that the child be old enough to have understanding. Understanding was by the parents. The child was to be embraced and contained under the name of God's people.

Reference has been made to the fact that parents were asked to reaffirm their faith, when presenting their child for baptism, by repeating the Apostles' Creed. In Knox's Book of Common Order there was a lengthy exposition of the Creed in which the parents were instructed and were reminded of the historic faith of the believing community. Parents were reminded also that their child was involved in the predicament of the human family; that he inherited a sinful nature; that he needed the cleansing power of the Holy Spirit, of which water is the scriptural emblem; that they as parents were to live worthily and manifest their godly fear before the child; and that they were to instruct the child, pray with

him and for him, and bring him up in the nurture and admonition
of the Lord. He reminded the members of the congregation that it
was important for them to be present when children were presented for baptism, for this was an occasion in which God would
speak to them through the sacrament. Parents were asked to take encouragement, knowing that God watches over their children. After
the service of baptism the minister was expected to say, "I receive
this child into the fellowship of the church." Thus, the child of the
covenant was a part of the church and had a right to receive the
pastoral care, the oversight, and the instruction the church provided for all members of the congregation.

Knox held a very strong view of the sacraments. He emphasized
the activities of God, through the Holy Spirit, when the sacraments
were observed. He regarded the proper administration of the
sacraments as the proclamation of the gospel: "And thus we utter-
lie dampne the vanitie of those that affirme Sacramentis to be
nothing else but naked and bair signes. No, we assuredlie beleve,
that by Baptisme we ar ingrafted in Christ Jesus to be maid parta-
karis of his justice, by the whiche our synes are covered and re-
mitted; and also, that in the Supper, rychtlie used, Christ Jesus is
so joyned with us, that he becumis the verray nurishement and
foode of our saullis."[21]

Another observation follows which is of encouragement to the
faithful. To provide for times when it appears that the sacraments
have had no effect upon one who observes Communion, Knox
writes: "Yit shall it after bring furth frute, as livelie seid sawin in
good ground; for the Holy Spreit, whiche can never be devided
frome the rycht institutioun of the Lord Jesus, will not frustrat the
faythefull of the frute of that misticall actioun."[22]

Concern for the Poor

The responsibility of the church for the poor was emphasized
in Knox's ministry and writings. In the Book of Discipline it was
stated that the church should care for the poor. Funds for this
ministry, as well as for public education, were expected to come
from the vast possessions accumulated in Scotland by the Roman
Church. This plan failed, as we have seen. The lords of the land

said they did not want to see the wealth of the church dissipated by the Reformers' "devout imaginations."

Knox was aware of problems in administering help to the poor. In the Book of Discipline he stated that if a man was strong he was to engage in work or he would not receive help from the church. The needy were to be returned to the district from which they came, where their own people were expected to care for them. Such views remind us that the life of a believer and the life of the church were not to be lived in a vacuum. Christian faith calls for compassion that acts. The meaning of love is reflected and taught through deeds. The whole of man is to be ministered to by the church.

The Gospel Is Concerned About Life in the State

The reader's familiarity with the history of Knox and of the struggle between the fiery Reformer and Mary Queen of Scots will enable him to recall the strong views Knox held on the prophetic role of the minister of the gospel. He did not hesitate to inject the word of the preacher into the political situation of his day. In the "First Blast of the Trumpet Against the Monstruous Regiment of Women" he vehemently denounced the reign of women on the throne. He contended that women ought never to exercise authority over men or be heard to speak in the congregation of the church. It ought to be said that during Knox's life he had ample reasons to denounce the cruel despotism of women rulers. He knew the wrath of Mary Tudor, of England, and Mary of Guise, Regent of Scotland, as well as the fierce determination of Mary Queen of Scots to overthrow the Reformation of which Knox was the acknowledged leader. Knox's audience with her is known to every student of English history. He believed the voice of the clergy should be heard on matters of government and particularly on the conduct of rulers. He marshaled the forces of the state, disorganized as they were, in opposition to Rome and the Crown as they united to stamp out the Reformation. While he believed the church should have exclusive right to state her theology and write her discipline, he believed that the disciplines of the church should be enforced by the state.

Knox believed the Crown to be an instrument of God. He stood for obedience to law. He opposed the practices current in Scotland of men taking the law into their own hands and gaining vengeance upon their adversaries. At the same time Knox believed that the Crown and government had a responsibility to their people, that government which was corrupt or contrary to the Word of God was to be opposed and, if needs be, overthrown. He boldly stated this to the Queen Dowager and later to Mary Queen of Scots. To the Queen Regent he wrote: "For better, we think, to expose our bodies to a thousand deaths, than to hazard our souls to perpetual condemnation by denying Christ Jesus and his manifest verity."[23]

The stern leader of the Reformation was infuriated when the Queen Regent, after promising religious moderation, tolerance, and freedom, retracted the promise and attempted the arrest of the Reformers in Scotland. In a message to be delivered by a group of Scottish lords he said: "I most humbly require of you, my Lords, in my name, to say to the Queen's Grace Regent, that we, whom she in her blind rage doth persecute, are God's servants, faithful and obedient subjects to the authority of this realm . . . I further require your Honours, in my name, to say unto her Grace . . . that this her enterprise shall not prosperously succeed in the end . . . for she fighteth not against man only, but against the eternal God and his invincible verity."[24]

It is strikingly clear in Knox's words and works that he considered the government, and the kind of life lived by those who exercised government, to be a matter of concern and responsibility to the church and her pastors. The separation of church and state is sometimes interpreted to mean that the church should keep silent when there are great moral and social issues involved. This would be in sharp contrast with the views taken and practiced by Knox. His view was that the church should be concerned about the redemption of society, collectively as well as individually. Martin Luther was concerned about the salvation of the individual. John Calvin was concerned about the salvation of a city. Knox was concerned about the salvation of a nation.

Knox's success in Scotland was due to his clear understanding of the issues involved, his uncanny insight into the meaning of the events of history in his day, his strong convictions regarding the truth and authority of the Scriptures, and his powerful gifts as a speaker. No man in Scotland could arouse a congregation or audience in that day as could this dark-eyed, fiery preacher. It cannot be said that the tremendous success he had was due to his preaching alone, or to the emphasis he placed upon teaching the Word of God, or to his political leadership of the lords of Scotland, or to his sincerity. Together, however, such qualities made him effective to a degree few men have equaled. All that one is and does teaches and proclaims the gospel he believes. Christian nurture, in the life and works of Knox, is what the term implies. It is the church engaged in teaching the faith entrusted to it through proclamation, worship, instruction, nurture in the home, ministry in society, and involvement in the life of the nation. It is teaching the whole gospel to the whole of man in the whole of society.

4 | THE ROAD
WE HAVE TRAVELED

The Presbyterian Church in the United States (then of the Confederate States of America) was constituted in Augusta, Georgia, December 4, 1861. One must turn to the history of the early settlers in the Colonies and trace their roots back to the Reformation Churches in Europe to understand the viewpoints expressed in the doctrines and practices of the Presbyterian Church. Settlers who came from Holland, France, Scotland, England, Germany, Switzerland, and Ireland brought with them their unique theological views and concepts of the Christian faith. If the United States is composed of a population amalgamated from the peoples of the earth, the Presbyterian Church in the United States is an amalgamation of the Presbyterian and Reformed Churches of Europe.

The New England States were settled by the Puritans. Although many of them practiced the congregational form of church government, they were Calvinists in their theology. Their concepts of life were influenced greatly by the Puritans of England, who practiced and taught a strict code of conduct. There was a legalistic attitude toward ethical and moral standards, and severe punishment was inflicted upon those who violated the moral code or laws governing the Sabbath. The behavior of "boys who met girls" was strictly circumscribed. Piety was measured largely by strict adherence to standards established by the Puritans. There is a lingering effect of this background in the life of Presbyterians today, reflected in the view that to refrain from certain practices on Sunday, to dress in a certain manner, and to give up certain pleasures, particularly the theatre, are marks of Christian piety.

Settlers from Scotland came in great numbers to the Carolinas, Pennsylvania, and sections of Virginia. They had passed through the agonizing experience of wresting religious and political freedom from the Catholic hierarchy, Mary of Guise, Mary Queen of Scots, and the English Crown. The blood of men like Patrick Hamilton, George Wishart, John Knox, and Andrew Melville was in their veins. They brought with them the belief that the church was to be separated from government control. They believed they should be free to use the Bible as an open book. They believed that schools and colleges should be established by the church. Heads of families were held responsible for teaching the Christian faith to their children. These concepts have been basic in the life and work of the Presbyterian Church.

French Huguenots settled in the Carolinas. They had fled from France after the Edict of Nantes. Along with the descendants of Presbyterians of Scotland, they opposed the interference of the state in matters of religion.

From Switzerland, Germany, and the British Isles came those who were familiar with doctrines taught by Calvin, Bucer, Bullinger, Zwingli, Melanchthon, Knox, Tyndale, and Coverdale. They came from churches that had adopted standards and articles of faith and were aware of the evil effects of false doctrines in the church. It is quite understandable that the catechisms and doctrinal standards of the European churches from which early settlers in America came would constitute the basis of standards accepted and taught in churches in the Colonies.

Francis Makemie was not the first Presbyterian minister who came to the new world, but he is justly called the "Father of Presbyterianism in America." He was only twenty-five years of age when he landed in Maryland. He immediately began to organize Presbyterian churches. He traveled from New York to Georgia, often suffering religious persecution from the early settlers.

The first presbytery in the new world was the Presbytery of Philadelphia, which was constituted in 1706. The first synod was constituted in 1717. It was not until 1729 that the doctrinal standards of the Westminster Confession of Faith and the Larger and

Shorter Catechisms were adopted as the standards of American Presbyterianism. The first General Assembly was constituted in 1788, with four synods. Two of the synods were Virginia and the Carolinas.

Those were hard days for the settlers, many of whom moved from the coast to the mountains and across the mountains into the hinterland of this great continent. The church could not, or did not, always follow them. Education lagged. Slavery was introduced. The economy of the nation brought a great influx of slaves into the South. Sectionalism developed, and religious and political disputes and divisions arose. Signs of an impending political storm appeared. The embers of pride, bitterness, and sectionalism were fanned into a fire that broke upon the land in consuming fury. The political division of the Confederate States resulted. The Gardiner Spring Resolutions that called upon all Presbyterians north and south to be loyal to the Federal government and support it were adopted by the 1861 General Assembly. Presbyterians in the Confederate States could not accept these resolutions. They withdrew from the Assembly and organized the Presbyterian Church in the Confederate States of America.

Foundations of Christian Education

The foundations of Christian education in the Presbyterian Church in the United States are derived from several sources. Apart from the Bible, which is basic and central, the primary source of the concepts of Christian nurture is found in the doctrinal standards of the church. The Westminster Confession of Faith and the Larger and Shorter Catechisms, adopted when the Assembly was constituted in 1861, together with the Book of Church Order officially adopted in 1879, contain the theological bases of the teachings and beliefs of the church. Brief statements of faith have been adopted, first in 1913 and again in 1962. But the Westminster Standards contain the substance of the doctrines the church has preached and taught.

There has been, in the church, a strong emphasis upon loyalty to doctrinal standards. Ministers have been examined on their views, and if there was doubt as to their loyalty to the standards of the church, membership in a presbytery was withheld until they were willing to subscribe to them. It has not always been enough that ministers subscribe to the Westminster Standards "as containing the system of doctrine taught in the Holy Scriptures."[1] There have been instances in which church courts have required assent to an exact doctrinal position held by members of the court. Some ministers and presbyteries have insisted upon belief in a particular theory of the inspiration of the Scriptures, indicating that one could not be sound in the faith unless he believed in the theory of verbal inspiration. Belief in the authority of the Scriptures has been equated with belief in the inerrancy of the Scriptures. Such views are inconsistent with the views on the authority of the Scriptures held by Calvin and Knox.

The first General Assembly clearly indicated its conviction that the church was thoroughly committed to the missionary task. This concept has been kept before the church and represents one of its great passions. It has influenced her work and her education. It is tragic that the church that bodily declared its intention of preaching the gospel to all people and all nations has not lived by the conviction expressed. All races of people overseas have been served by missionaries of the church. But in the states and communities within the bounds of the Assembly the story is quite different.

There was another theological view of that day that has affected our concepts of preaching and teaching. The doctrine of "the church" is a subject of prime importance. Benjamin Palmer, of New Orleans, preached the opening sermon of the Constituting Assembly. His subject was "The Headship of Christ over the Church." In emphasizing the fact that Christ, and not Caesar, is the head of the church he indicated that the mission of the church is purely spiritual, and not in any sense political. The "Address to All the Churches of Jesus Christ Throughout the Earth," prepared by a committee and reported and read by Dr. James H. Thornwell, emphasized this position. In 1866 the Assembly adopted a resolution that began, "In view of the great controversy now pending in this country, upon the spirituality and independence of the Church as the visible kingdom of the Lord Jesus Christ . . . "[2] In dealing with what was undoubtedly a crucial issue of that day, the presentation of the concept of the church as being purely spiritual has had a lasting effect upon the Presbyterian Church in the United States.

Ernest Trice Thompson, former Moderator of the Assembly, has written a book entitled *The Spirituality of the Church*. In it he traces the origin and history of this doctrine in the Presbyterian Church. The views developed as Presbyterian pastors joined Southern statesmen in facing the moral issues connected with the slave traffic.

Following the Revolutionary War, there was a period of strong antislavery sentiment. Slavery as an institution was recognized as wrong, and churches made deliverances against its evils. Three of the largest Protestant bodies—Methodist, Baptist, and Presbyterian—spoke out against it. However, they were not united in the belief that the church as an organized body should deal with the issue. John Holt Rice, in 1827, wrote to a friend: "I am most fully convinced that slavery is the greatest evil in our country, except whiskey; and it is my most ardent prayer that we may be delivered from it. . . . The reason why I am so strenuously opposed to any movement by the church or the ministers of religion on the subject is simply this. I am convinced that any thing we can do will injure religion, and retard the march of public feeling in relation to slavery. . . . as slavery exists among us, the only possible chance of deliverance is by *making the people willing* to get rid of it."[3] There it is. The conviction was that the problems of society were to be dealt with on the basis of personal conversion; that the church collectively should not be involved in a movement to correct the evil that was denounced. "I have long had it as an object dearest to my heart, to get Virginia free from slavery. I feel that the direct exertions of the church hinder the work,"[4] said Dr. Rice.

Before the organizing Assembly met in 1861, however, Southern opinion regarding slavery had changed drastically. Abolitionists in the North, both secular and religious, became venomous in their denunciation of slaveholders, and some evangelists insisted that they should be put out of the church.

Southern statesmen and ministers defended the South, and

eventually they began to justify the institution of slavery. The 1861 Assembly therefore did not definitely state that slavery was an evil to be corrected. Instead, it said: "We cannot but accept it as a gracious providence that they [the Negroes] have been brought in such numbers to our shores and redeemed from the bondage of barbarism and sin. Slavery to them has certainly been overruled for the general good. As long as that race in its comparative degradation exists side by side with the white, bondage is its natural condition."[5] A great theologian of the day, James Henley Thornwell, said, "We stand upon the platform of the Bible. God's Word recognizes the relation of master and servants as a relation that may lawfully subsist." As a spiritual body, the church, he proceeded to argue, "has no right to interfere directly with the civil relations of society. . . . [The church] is not a moral institute of universal good, whose business it is to wage war upon every form of human ill . . . It has no commission to construct society afresh . . . to change the forms of its political constitutions." The solution of such problems was to be left "to the Providence of God, and to human wisdom sanctified and guided by the spiritual influences which it is her glory to foster and to cherish."[6]

A list of the leaders of the church of that day who held to the general concept that the church was to be engaged in a spiritual task apart from and unrelated to the actions of society and the state would include such men as B. M. Palmer, J. B. Adger, J. L. Girardeau, Thomas E. Peck, and Robert L. Dabney—the giants of the church. There was no lack of integrity in these illustrious theologians nor any lack of courage in the "prophets of God" of their era. The facts of history simply affirm that the Presbyterian Church in the United States came into existence in the context of a social climate that thought the church was not to be involved in issues and actions of the social order or of the state. This view of the separation of religious truth from the culture and pattern of man's life has been accepted and has often resulted in preaching and teaching that were anemic and colorless. The clear implications of the great prophetic preaching of the Old Testament were, for a long time, seldom heard. The relevance of the teachings of Christ and the Epistles of Paul to the social issues of the day was not clearly recognized. When there were those who dealt with these issues, in either preaching or teaching, the comment often was, "We want a spiritual message," or "He is teaching a social gospel."

The Historical Development of Christian Education

The work of Christian education in the Presbyterian Church in the United States can be said to have begun in August, 1862, with the appearance of the first printed material prepared by the Executive Committee of Publication. This was a paper called *The Children's Friend*. Three thousand copies were printed. This supply was soon exhausted, and ten thousand additional copies were prepared. The materials were for children. If there was any effort to provide instruction for adults, there is no record of it. Nor was there any great emphasis upon the education of youth. Christian education was for children. The lesson material was in the form of questions on biblical content. The first studies were of four books of the Bible—Matthew, Mark, Acts, and Hebrews.

The Executive Committee, of which Moses D. Hoge was chairman, had a deep interest in providing Bibles for men in the army of the Confederacy. Through Dr. Hoge's determined leadership, Bibles and Testaments were secured from England and placed in the hands of the soldiers. The church welcomed this opportunity to offer nurture and comfort to those on the battlefield.

During the Civil War the Committee went through some dark days. In 1865 the city of Richmond was burned. All of the plates and cuts owned by the Committee were destroyed. For a brief time the publication of materials ceased. But out of the ashes and sorrows of those days came a new determination to edit and print materials for Christian education.

In the early history of the church no special materials were prepared for youth. Material for adults was for their use as teachers of children. In October, 1870, the *Earnest Worker* was first printed. For nearly a hundred years this teachers' quarterly has been one of the most popular and widely used pieces of material the Committee has published. In 1870 the *Earnest Worker* contained expositions of lesson passages, articles on the importance of lesson preparation by the teacher, materials for teachers and superintendents, some suggestions on ways of conducting classes, and questions on the Bible lessons for particular Sundays. The questions were on three age levels—for young children, intermediates, and teachers. Lesson helps for the pupil were in the form of questions.

In 1875, after extensive debate in the General Assembly, the Committee was authorized to publish material that led eventually to production of the International Uniform Lessons. In reporting the proposed co-operation with the Reformed Church in America, the Assembly Minutes stated that the *Earnest Worker* and two Reformed papers would merge and become one paper. The report continued: "This scheme carries with it necessarily the publication of the International Series of Sabbath Lessons."[7]

Opposition to the International series was based on the fear that the theological viewpoints would not be consistent with the standards of the Presbyterian Church, and that the Committee would lose control of its editorial work. There was much truth in the view that the materials chosen by representatives of many denominations would not permit planning of lessons that would emphasize distinctive doctrines of the denominations. On the other hand, the element of strength in the International series was the spirit of co-operation this lesson planning introduced into the denominations producing them. It was one of the first movements toward ecumenical fellowship among the Protestant Churches in the United States. Doctrines objectionable to certain denominations were usually avoided. Such subjects as the Lord's Supper, the mode of baptism, form of church government, and predestination were minimized or omitted. Of course, denominational writers and editors had the freedom to teach and expound such doctrines. But a biblical study of these doctrines was not included in the outlines of the International Uniform Lessons.

When in 1875 the Committee formed its first association with the Reformed Church in America, the committees of these two churches entered into an agreement to co-operate in the publication of the *Earnest Worker. The Gospel Sower,* with a circulation of over 8,000 copies, took the place of the *Earnest Worker* for the year

1876, but as this joint periodical did not exactly meet the needs of either church, the *Earnest Worker* was revived on January 1, 1877.

About this time the Assembly authorized another periodical, to be of interest to small children. It finally appeared in early 1893, as a weekly story paper called *Pearls for the Little Ones*. Many of the stories were about missionaries and Christian leaders.

In 1883 the Assembly urged parents to go to Sunday school with their children. Parents were reminded that thus they would be teaching their children, by both precept and example, "to love and profit by the privileges here afforded them."

An interesting recommendation, acted upon favorably, is found in the minutes of the 1885 Assembly: "That the ministers and Sessions be encouraged to so enlarge the Sabbath-school and Bible-class instruction as to embrace as far as practicable the adult portion of the congregations, and train them for useful officers and workers in the Church."[8] The same emphasis was reflected the next year when the following recommendation was adopted: "To urge the church Sessions to use all diligence to secure the attendance of older persons on the Sunday-school, that the school may be what it ought to be, the church studying the Word of God."[9]

The first steps in the development of youth work appear to have been taken in 1892, when the Assembly was asked to approve the formation of "Young People's Societies." The Assembly appointed an ad interim committee to study the advisability of such an organization. The proposal evidently encountered many difficulties. The committee's report the following year was referred to a committee of five which submitted majority and minority reports to that Assembly. These reports were referred to another committee, and in 1894 approval finally was given for the organization of such societies, to be under the supervision and direction of their respective Sessions. Special concern was expressed that "In societies which are constituted of both sexes, sessions should take care that the women and girls do not transgress the limitations of Scripture by conducting meetings or by engaging in public prayer and exhortation."[10] These societies after 1895 usually carried the name recommended by the Assembly of that year—"Westminster League."

In 1896 a society for boys only was organized in the Second Presbyterian Church of Richmond under the name "Covenanter." Two years later the Miriam society for girls was formed in the same church. News of these organizations spread to other congregations, and similar groups resulted. The Assembly in 1896 directed the Executive Committee of Publication to have prepared for the use of "the Westminster Leagues, or Young People's Societies of our church," a series of topics for study. Earlier a word of caution had been included in the Constitution of the Westminster Leagues: they were to refrain from association with youth groups that were antagonistic or unfriendly toward the system of doctrine and government of the Presbyterian Church. (In 1897 the Assembly consented to the deletion of this paragraph.) By 1904 the Committee could report that 109 Covenanter companies and eight Miriam chapters had been enrolled. Both groups were said to be "essentially missionary in organization and work."[11]

The second major period in the development of Christian education began in 1904. The first period, from 1861 to 1904, was marked by the preparation of educational material by the Committee, a program centered in the education of children, a recognition of the importance of training teachers, the beginning of youth work, and first signs of the development of adult classes. Bible classes for adults had been proposed as a means of training Sunday school teachers and leaders.

In 1904 the Assembly authorized the Committee to call a staff member who would have the title of General Superintendent of Sabbath Schools and Young People's Societies. His assignment was to develop a planned program of Christian education. The next fifty years were to witness the rapid development of Christian education. The program would provide for the educational needs of most, if not all, of the congregation, including children and youth of the community. It would offer educational opportunities through such activities as vacation church schools, extended sessions of the Sunday school, youth conferences, camps, conferences for men, extensive leadership training, and the many other types of activities characteristic of the educational work of the church during the first half of the twentieth century.

It was in the early part of the twentieth century that references to the organization of adult Bible classes appeared. The report of the Executive Committee of Publication and Sabbath School Work to the 1905 Assembly recommended a special effort to organize "Young Men and Young Women's Bible Classes" in October of that year. Adults were encouraged to attend Sunday school and to engage in home study of the Sunday school lessons. Evidently the time was ripe for adult classes, for from 1906 to 1930 the establishment of adult classes is one of the significant developments in Christian education. Adults studied the International Uniform Lessons. With the enrollment and attendance of adults, the entire Sunday school movement took on new proportions. Children and young people came in increasing numbers, and as adults received training in Bible study the quality of teaching improved.

Until this time, little consideration had been given to methods of teaching. In adult classes lectures were used most frequently. There were the exceptional instances of teachers who asked questions, or who requested class members to report on an assignment. Men and women were in separate classes.

During the first forty years of the twentieth century, organized classes began to function as if they were churches. Using fixed orders of worship, men's Bible classes duplicated many features of the eleven o'clock service of worship. Emphasis was placed upon singing and music. Offerings were received and disbursed according to budgets prepared by class officers.

Many of these Bible classes had a strong evangelistic program and appeal. In some cities, after nationally known evangelists conducted lengthy revivals, independent or nondenominational Bible classes were established. These were not related to the church and usually were promoted by laymen who wished to perpetuate the activities of the revival. Too often, members of those large Bible classes had no further connection with the church. After Sunday school was over, the men went their own way. It was an unwholesome theology and practice.

There were two other significant developments among adults during this period. The first of these was the organization of women. The training of women in Bible study, in the work of the church, and in forms of Christian service has had a value in their lives and in the life of the denomination which is beyond reckoning. One of the trends in the organized structure of the Women of the Church was toward a "little church within the church," although this had not been the intention of the Committee on Woman's Work (later the Board of Women's Work). It resulted from the zeal of the women and the lethargy of the men.

The Laymen's Missionary Movement, endorsed by the 1907 Assembly, was the first evidence of the awakened interest of men in the organized work of the church. The cause of missions received a healthy impetus through conferences for men in various sections of the church and through interdenominational missionary conventions held within the bounds of the Assembly. Giving to missions increased, and men were asked to promote stewardship in the church for the support of this cause. By 1922 men in local congregations were being organized to promote not only missions but all the causes of the church. Beginning about 1940 there were experiments in starting presbytery and synod organizations, and by 1950 the Division of Men's Work of the Board of Christian Education was established. The purpose of Men's Work was to enlist, motivate, and train men in the Christian life and in the life and work of the church. Today, men are engaged in studies of many kinds, including theology, social problems, and church officer training. They are examining the nature of Christian vocation. Men believe they are called to be Christians and to bear witness to their faith in and through their vocations. They are interested in a gospel that is relevant to all of life. The pattern of men's organization in the Presbyterian Church in the United States has been adapted for use by men in our armed forces. Their organization is called "Men of the Chapel."

In its report to the 1911 General Assembly the Committee dealt in detail with the recurring question of whether to use the "New Graded International Lesons" in addition to the established Uniform series. That year the committee "earnestly recommended" that the Assembly approve the continued use of the Uniform lesson system, and in 1912 the Committee's report again called attention to the danger of the new Graded Lessons, with their "insidious heresies." But the demand of the church became so strong that on January 1, 1915, the Committee began publication of the entirely new Departmental Graded Lessons, prepared through the joint editorial management of the Presbyterian Church in the U.S.A., the Presbyterian Church, U.S., the Canadian Presbyterian Church, the Reformed Church in America, the Reformed Church in the U.S., and the United Presbyterian Church. These materials were welcomed by the church, and subsequent reports indicated that they in no way lessened the circulation of the Uniform Lessons, as Sunday school enrollment was increasing steadily.

During the 1920's important changes in Christian education resulted from new insights and approaches to education by secular educators. Studies in psychology, patterns of behavior, the development of the individual, and the social sciences resulted in a philosophy of education popularly known as "progressive education." For the first time, those responsible for Christian education began to take notice of specific interests, concerns, and capacities of the growing person. Builders of curricula not only took notice of these factors but were practically swept away by them. Less emphasis was placed upon content and greater emphasis upon methodology. Curriculum became person-centered. The training of teachers meant training in educational methods and in an understanding of the person.

Among most of the denominations in the United States the educational program of the church was known as "religious education." It reflected a desire to recognize the values of all religious groups and to share with and receive from them new insights found in education. It was symptomatic of a humanistic approach to knowledge of God and growth in faith.

Goals and Objectives of Christian Education

The goals and objectives of Christian education represent the theological viewpoint characteristic of particular periods in the historical development of the church. They also reflect the educational concepts of the church and the culture of the particular periods of time in which noticeable changes occurred.

During the early years of the Presbyterian Church, U.S., the

primary objective was to teach the Bible to children. There seems
to have been no plan for systematic instruction. Some books of the
Old Testament were taught and some New Testament books were
taught, but there was little effort to show the relationship between
the Testaments or the interrelationship of the books of the Bible.
Teachers were expected to know the theological views of the denomination, and articles on Calvinistic doctrine were carried in the
Earnest Worker from time to time. Children were encouraged to
memorize the Shorter Catechism because it contained a summary
of the doctrines stated in the Confession of Faith.

From 1886 to 1911, articles in the *Earnest Worker* listed some
of the objectives for the teacher. The teacher was to know the
pupil, know the lesson, bring the lesson fairly within the pupil's
mental realm, secure and hold his attention, and arouse him to activity. Such goals for the teacher implied some knowledge of teaching methods, but little help in ways of teaching was offered during
those years.

By 1929, the Departmental Graded Lessons published by the
Committee had a circulation almost as large as that of the Uniform
series. The Junior and Primary materials in the Departmental
Graded series had been revised in accordance with the then current goals of religious education. The units around which the materials were organized reflected these goals. Six other denominations worked with members of the Committee staff in the revision.

The basic goals, as stated in that year, included a knowledge of
God the Father as Creator of the universe; of Jesus as the Son of
God and Savior of man; of the Holy Spirit and of God's presence
in the Holy Spirit; a willingness to make the ideals of the Father-
hood of God and the brotherhood of man a reality in experience;
a growing willingness and ability to participate in the work of the
organized church; the Christian interpretation of the universe and
of God's purpose; and an increasing knowledge of the Bible as the
inspired word of God.

These goals represented a shifting of emphasis from a body of
materials to be studied to a growing person whose spiritual needs
were to be met. Bible passages that bore upon the goals were
chosen—chapters of the Bible, portions of chapters, and selected

verses. There was a clear statement of the desired outcomes of teaching, the treatment was more comprehensive, and Bible study was supported by related worship materials and learning activities.

In 1945 another major step was taken when the Committee's working relationships with other denominations were broadened and the goals of Christian education were improved and strengthened. New outlines prepared in co-operation with a large interdenominational group were then reworked to accord with the doctrinal position and particular needs of our church. That year, beginning in October, a new cycle of Graded materials for Beginner, Primary, and Junior children was ready for use. Bible study was simplified, and teaching plans were adapted to schools of all sizes and circumstances.

Much can be said in favor of the concepts of Christian education during this period of the church's life. To study the Bible merely to master scriptural content is not the ultimate objective of Bible study. Nor should the indoctrination of believers in the orthodox creeds of the church be the ultimate aim of instruction in theology. Theology has a relevancy to life. This relevancy often had been ignored in the teaching program of earlier years. There was a need to have the beliefs of the church find expression in character and daily life. The church was still suffering, however, from the doctrine that the nature of the church is "purely spiritual." The church was not involved in the ethical, social, and moral issues people faced every day.

On the whole, progressive education had a healthy effect upon religious education even though some of the emphases were not consistent with the nature of revelation and our understanding of how man comes to know God. Religious education during the period from 1929 to 1950 helped the church to break out of some very limited concepts of the Christian faith and of how Christian nurture takes place. The importance of living the Christian faith, as well as learning about it, was recognized. A strong emphasis upon working to establish the Kingdom of God in the world in which man lives was accompanied by new concepts of brotherhood.

As man's knowledge of science increased, old views about the creation of the world in a literal "six days" were seen to be inconsistent with discoveries in astronomy and geology. Therefore, theologians and Bible scholars were compelled to re-examine the teachings of the Bible to discover what God has been saying all through the centuries.

At times the emphasis upon a gospel that demands social righteousness and calls upon men to become involved in the struggles for justice, economic practices that are honest and fair, the improvement of housing and the environment in which people live, was so vigorous and persistent that the church was accused of being concerned about social and economic reforms rather than about preaching and teaching the "pure gospel." Yet it was important that the limited concepts of religious education be broken and a truer understanding of the gospel be reached and taught.

There were some decided weaknesses in the religious education emphases of this period. The Bible was presented from a preconceived viewpoint. Little opportunity was given for study that would allow the Bible to speak its own message under the guidance of the Holy Spirit. Passages that supported such objectives as kindness, honesty, obedience to civil authority, and virtuous living were selected and studied with these goals in mind. The issue was not that such goals were less than Christian, but that the results of Bible study were too largely predetermined.

Another weakness of the Bible study of this period was that the passages studied were fragmentary. The importance of specific Bible events, stories, and major sections of biblical content was not recognized. Little attention was given to the unity of the Scriptures, wherein teachings and doctrines set forth in one section are related to similar teachings in other passages of the Bible. Often neglected, too, was the unfolding story of God's dealings with his people, the establishing of his covenant with man, the purposes of God reflected in the unfolding story, and the eschatological hope of the Christian community. The approach to man's understanding of God was from the viewpoint of man. It was a humanistic approach, in which man discovers, finds, understands, becomes aware of, and lays hold upon God, rather than the biblical doctrine of revelation, in which God takes the initiative and lays hold upon man.

Another shortcoming of the curriculum building of this time was the lack of over-all planning. The Graded outlines of study for children were developed independently of outlines of study for young people. The outlines of study for adults were based upon Uniform Lesson outlines and were completely apart from the Graded curriculum for either children or youth.

Very little in the way of new studies for adults was offered. The Uniform Lessons continued year after year, cycle after cycle. Great as were the advantages of using the International Uniform Lessons—such advantages as having syndicated lessons helps in the daily papers, interdenominational use of the lessons, and dated materials that could be followed with ease—the disadvantages were apparent also. Adults were faced with a new world and new conditions which were not always taken into consideration in the Uniform cycles. Helps were needed in areas the Uniform material did not cover. Elective studies began to be used. But again the development of adult lessons was not so much by plan as it was by long-established patterns and by the reluctance of adults to break away from old patterns of Sunday school lectures and classes.

It was most unfortunate that theologians and pastors, in the first forty years of the twentieth century, did not help shape religious education in the United States. There were exceptions, of course, but theological seminaries continued to emphasize the basic theological disciplines. The twentieth century was far advanced before departments or chairs of religious education appeared. Pastors believed that laymen should direct and develop the program of religious education. It was proper that laymen should be deeply involved in the work, but pastors should not have been allowed to forfeit their responsibilities. As a result of the neglect of religious education by those who were trained in theology there was too little instruction in doctrines, creeds, and catechisms.

In the beginning of the Sunday school movement there was a strong emphasis upon the nature and importance of evangelism. One of the purposes of the Sunday school was to "evangelize." Pupils were to be encouraged to confess their faith in Christ as Savior and Lord. Teachers were instructed to sound the note of urgency for pupils to confess Christ. Christian education was defined as "education to evangelize."

The Executive Committee sought to fulfill its role in educational evangelism through the establishment of new Sunday schools. It brought to its staff from fifteen to twenty-five persons, men and women, who engaged in the organization of new Sunday schools. Almost every presbytery had in it some persons whose ministry included, in addition to that of his own congregation or group of churches, the work of Sunday School Evangelism in the presbytery. This included the establishment of new Sunday schools. The Committee spent a great proportion of its budget for this work, which was really "Home Missions." It should be noted that this was a time when the church grew very rapidly.

Because of the concentration upon the importance of evangelism, Christian nurture or Christian growth often had a secondary role. Those who preach and teach must of course be concerned about the salvation of individuals. A teacher in the church school can be of great help to those in the class who need to gain a clear understanding of the meaning of faith, of the work of Christ the Redeemer, of the necessity to repent of sin and to trust in Christ. But to make evangelism the only emphasis of a class causes an imbalance. Those who already have a saving faith are to grow in knowledge, in wisdom, in faith, and in Christlikeness.

The concept of "evangelism as the sole goal of the church school" has resulted, in some instances, in a program of "Child Evangelism" that often persuades children to profess what is beyond them. Children are encouraged to do what they are not by nature and age prepared to do.

This strong emphasis upon the evangelism of children through a "crisis decision by children" is, in a sense, a denial of the doctrine of the covenant. The Standards of the Presbyterian Church, U. S., state that "children of believing parents are members of the Church." True, they are not communing members, but they are members of the covenant family. They have a right to the ministry, instruction, love, and care of the church.

The importance of educating children and youth in the work and program of the church has been recognized throughout the history of the Presbyterian Church. When plans were made to build a steamboat, name it the *Samuel N. Lapsley* for a pioneer missionary, and use it to transport our missionaries and others living in the Belgian Congo, Sunday school children were informed of the need and were encouraged to give their pennies and nickels and dimes so that the boat could be purchased. In 1894 the Assembly commended "the successful effort of the children to raise ten thousand dollars to build a steamboat for use on the Congo River in Africa." This project had provided excellent training. It made the cause of missions vivid, specific, and interesting. One of the ironies of the church, however, was that while children were encouraged to give to reach the people of Africa in Africa, less and less was done for those of African descent who live in our midst. If Negroes came to church they were expected to sit in a remote section of the sanctuary, preferably the balcony.

It has not been easy for the Assembly to reach a clear decision as to the implications of the gospel for the Negro in our midst. There was a clearer note sounded in a report made to the 1865 Assembly than will be found in many later actions of the Assembly. That year the Assembly stated its conviction that "Whereas, the colored people never stood in any other relation to the Church than that of human beings lost with us in the fall of Adam; and redeemed with us by the infinitely meritorious death and sacrifice of Christ, and participants with us in all the benefits and blessings of the Gospel; and whereas our churches, pastors, and people have always recognized this claim to Christian equality and brotherhood, and have rejoiced to have them associated in Christian union and communion in the public services and precious sacraments of the sanctuary:

"Resolved, 1st, That the abolition of slavery by the civil and military powers, has not altered the relations as above defined, in which our Church stands to the colored people, nor in any degree lessened the debt of love and service which we owe to them, nor the interest with which we would still desire to be associated with them in all the privileges of our common Christianity.

"Resolved, 2nd, That whereas experience has invariably proved the advantages of the colored people and the white being united together in the worship of God, we see no reason why it should be otherwise . . ."

The report went on to say that "Should our colored friends think it best to separate from us, and organize themselves into distinct congregations," the church would do all in its power to encourage and assist them, providing white pastors and elders until God should raise up colored elders and pastors "suitably qualified for those offices."[12] One of the greatest preachers of the day, Dr. John L. Girardeau, devoted a large part of his ministry to preaching to Negroes in Charleston, South Carolina. In 1907 all ministers of the church were urged by the Assembly to preach at least one sermon a month to Negro congregations within their bounds.

In due time, Negro presbyteries were organized—one in 1876, and the next in 1890. A Negro synod, organized in 1916, voted the next year to be called Snedecor Memorial, in recognition of the work of Rev. J. G. Snedecor, who for thirteen years served the Assembly in connection with Colored Evangelization. The establishment of Tuscaloosa Institute, for the education of Negroes, was authorized by the Assembly in 1876, and in 1894 the name was changed to Stillman in honor of its first superintendent. But in spite of the fine work among Negroes done by many Presbyterian ministers and members through the years, the work has never been as fruitful as it should have been.

It was during the first part of the twentieth century that many churches made it clear that they would not welcome Negroes in their congregations. Of course, the faithful servants, beloved Negro nurses, and special Negro friends could attend church when some of their "white folks" were being married, or when there was a funeral. But the custom of bringing Negroes into the fellowship of the church, or even of allowing them to worship in the same sanctuary, gradually became impossible in many congregations. The church has permitted two generations to follow this pattern. The statement that the eleven o'clock service of worship in Protestant churches on Sunday morning is the most segregated hour in the week is not pleasant to hear, but the truth of it cannot be denied. Education less than Christian has resulted from the practice the church has followed. A church educates by the life it lives, by its practices, by its traditions, and by its willingness or unwillingness to face the full implications of the gospel.

In recent years the conscience, mind, and heart of the church have become awakened and aroused. The Assembly has approved some of the clearest and most forthright statements on Christian responsibilities toward all races, and particularly the Negro race, of any denomination in the United States. Leaders in seminaries have contributed significantly toward the correction of errors in the church's practices and supporting theology. The Board of Christian Education has accepted its role in teaching and promoting Christian responsibilities toward all men. A social revolution is taking place in the nation. The struggle is a difficult one. Harsh, unkind, and unjust things are said and done. Injustices are perpetrated. The Assembly has called upon its boards, agencies, colleges, and schools to recognize the dignity and worth of all persons and to deal justly with all. Sessions have been urged to receive people into the church only on the biblical basis of membership—repentance for sin and faith in Jesus Christ as Savior and Lord. The battle—and it must be called that—is against wrongs, injustice, and fierce forces of pride and animosity; and the battle continues. Successes have been achieved. Little Rock has its note of humiliation and shame. But Little Rock also has a story of many courageous Christians whose loving hearts and bold leadership have won notable victories.

The Reformed Churches have always stressed Christian ethics. In Calvin's ministry in Geneva, reform of conduct as well as reform of theology was demanded. Geneva was filled with every kind of vice imaginable. Calvin preached and taught the necessity for regeneration and reform. He advocated and practiced the most rigid standards of moral rectitude. Those who became Christians and united with the church were expected to manifest Christian righteousness. If they failed to do so they were disciplined. If they did not respond to discipline they were excommunicated. The City Council was asked to enact laws that forbade the open practice of immorality, intemperance, and loose living. John Knox in Scotland also emphasized the necessity for reformation in the life of church members. Knox's discipline was severe and harsh. But let this be said of Calvin and Knox: their concepts of ethics grew out of their understanding of the nature of the gospel. The ethical standards they taught were based upon their interpretation of Scripture.

Christian ethics grew out of the nature of God, his revelation to man, the nature of man, and man's relation to God.

This was the concept reflected in the preaching of church leaders in 1861 and the years that followed. Ethics to them meant first of all the demands of the gospel upon the life of the believer. The problem of conquering evil in life and securing proper conduct by man was to be solved by conversion and by Christ's establishing his rule over man. But our founding fathers of 1861 did not advocate the active involvement of the church in social and ethical problems.

Often in the hundred years of the denomination's life (and this was characteristic of Protestantism) there has been the tendency to emphasize secondary issues. This kept the church from dealing with basic matters. Much time was spent in discussion about card-playing, the manner of dress for women, forms of Sabbath desecration, and complete abstinence from alcoholic beverages. It was assumed that theatres—and later, moving pictures—were evil and not to be patronized. These matters undeniably involve ethical problems. But the peril of the church was that other more serious problems were overlooked, or were considered beyond the concern and responsibility of the church. Business monopolies were allowed to develop with little challenge by the church of the abuses and evils growing out of them. There was the great concentration of wealth—and widespread poverty. Child labor was permitted. Laborers were employed to work for twelve and fourteen hours a day at near starvation wages. Slums developed in cities, and hovels were common in villages and countryside. The growth of secularism continued in our social structure. Preachers were supposed to "preach a spiritual message," never to touch upon the social conditions that were constantly growing worse.

Confronted by society's urgent demand for the church's answer to these problems, and seeing the great needs for which the Holy Spirit calls us, the Board of Christian Education, in 1955, recognized that the time had come for a fresh approach to the church's understanding of its task in Christian nurture. The development of this idea has resulted in the Covenant Life Curriculum.

5 | COVENANT
LIFE CURRICULUM

A new curriculum of Christian education, called the Covenant Life Curriculum, is being offered in the Presbyterian Church in the United States and four other denominations which united in creating it.

The Origin of the New Curriculum

In 1955 the Board of Christian Education decided that the time had come for a study of its educational program. For several years prior to 1955, the staff of the Board had been engaged in special studies of subjects related to its work. New approaches to Bible study were examined. Attention was given to the importance of theology in the understanding of the faith. Great social changes had taken place in the nation and in the world since the Second World War. The explosion of the first atomic bomb marked the advent of a new age in science and government. God was leading the Presbyterian Church, U. S., into the ecumenical movement, already so clearly in evidence throughout the world. New means of communication had come into being and gave promise of reshaping the thoughts and lives of people everywhere. There was a population explosion. The race issue was growing in importance and since that time has become crucial. A new age called for a serious study of the task of the church. Has our understanding of the faith been adequate? Does our religious life have in it the qualities of depth and breadth? Such questions demanded an answer.

The first wave of religious enthusiasm that followed the Second World War had begun to recede. Service men and their families returning to their homes at the end of the war attended church in great numbers. Sunday schools experienced a remarkable numerical growth. The sincerity of those who attended church and Sunday school cannot be questioned, but there was reason to believe that a more serious approach to an understanding of the faith was essential. The small amount of time provided for study on Sunday morning hardly justified the term "education." Children and young people were irregular in attendance, and only a small proportion of adults were enrolled in Sunday schools. The content of Sunday school lesson material was called into question. As the Board considered its trust, it believed the time had come for a re-examination of its curriculum of Christian education. The basic approach to this problem was an effort to discover the essential nature of the task. What is Christian education? What are the bases on which it rests? What is the nature of the faith the church communicates? How is faith communicated?

The Board was determined to meet its responsibility by seeking answers to the questions raised and by taking whatever steps were required in order to create a sound and effective curriculum of Christian education. In consultation with the Boards of the denominations associated with it in the creating of such a curriculum, the Board appointed a committee of twenty-three competent scholars, theologians, and church leaders to undertake a study. The committee was asked to explore as they would, and to take as much time as necessary, to define what Christian education is and to describe the bases upon which Christian education should be developed in churches holding to the Reformed faith.

The committee engaged in intensive study for two years. The result was a paper entitled "Basic Presuppositions and Guiding Principles for the Educational Work of the Church," which was submitted by the committee as their report to the Board. The report was thoroughly analyzed and studied, not only by Board and staff members but also by teachers, pastors, and administrators throughout the Assembly. Acceptance and approval were so overwhelming that the Board and staff, aided by the four co-operating denominations, set about the preparation of a new curriculum of Christian education, based upon the principles outlined.

The Objective of the Covenant Life Curriculum

The purpose of Christian education is described in the "Basic Presuppositions" paper as follows: "The educational work of the church seeks to relate man to God and not to use God for man's ends, or simply to solve man's problems. In all phases of its work the church seeks to present God as one who confronts man face to face, calling for a thoroughgoing change dealing with sin at its depths and a surrender of man's will to the will of God and offering redemption and new life."[1] Here in a striking way the purpose of Christian education reflected in the Covenant Life Curriculum stands out in bold contrast to purposes stated by earlier educators. There have been times when educators thought the purpose of the church was to teach the content of the Scriptures and have the learner become thoroughly familiar with it. While biblical content is important, the goal of Christian education is not solely that the content of Scripture should be mastered. One could know the Bible and be able to quote much of it from memory and still fail to enter into new life through Christ. The memorization of the names of the kings of Israel and Judah, the names of the Apostles, and the names of the books of the Bible do not necessarily result in a new life in Christ.

It is highly desirable that Christians reflect the traits of character commonly regarded as Christlike. Children and young people do well to manifest fine qualities of character and to practice deeds of loving service. But there is something far more basic of purpose than to establish goals that children shall be unselfish, that youth shall be obedient to authority, and that adults shall be law-abiding citizens. The Covenant Life Curriculum deals with the basic need of man and the central reason for Christ's work on man's behalf. It believes that the purpose of Christian education is "to provide the context and the means through which persons can have an experience of God and through which they can come to accept salvation and life offered by him."[2] The purpose is stated in another way as follows: "That all persons may respond in faith to the call of God in Jesus Christ and be nurtured in the life of fellowship with him, that they may face all of life's relationships and responsibilities as children of God."[3]

Because the Covenant Life Curriculum is based on the belief that the purpose of Christian education is to relate men fully to God and then to their fellow men, it emphasizes the importance of telling the story of God and his mighty acts on man's behalf and of presenting the claim of God upon man. This is done in the belief that through the Holy Spirit man will surrender his will to God as he is confronted by the God of revelation. It is out of this redemptive relationship with God that man will enter into a true relationship with all men. If man fails to enter into that covenant relationship with God he remains outside the covenant of life.

The Setting of Christian Education

Christian education takes place in certain settings within the church's life. A broad statement would be that one can be nurtured in every setting of life. The world ever impinges upon the person. Man's life is shaped by his environment, his heritage, his vocation, the government of his land, and the total cultural structure of his age. However, there are three settings within the church in which special provisions can be made for communicating and learning the Christian faith. Christian nurture takes place in the home, in the worship and work of the church, and in the program of study the church offers through its schools.

The home is the basic institution of life. Life is shaped by the influence of the home more than by any other institution of society. God has placed upon the family the responsibility of passing on its faith to its children. The historic position of the Reformed Church is that the home has been given the responsibility of teaching those who live together in the ties of family life. The covenant of baptism affords an opportunity for the church to remind the parents of their responsibilities in connection with the religious nurture of their children. But before parents can teach the faith adequately they must know it by experience and by a study of its meaning. The Covenant Life Curriculum offers guidance and educational material for families, to lead them into deeper under-

standing of their faith and of the meaning of faith for their life together. Because each member of the family has particular needs
which can be met only as each member of the family understands
the gospel, books interpreting the message of the gospel for family
situations are made available. Because family relationships exist in
a wide variety of patterns, books for the family are varied in content as well as purpose.

Those who are about to enter into the ties of marriage are offered guidance through books that explain the meaning of marriage from the viewpoint of the Word of God. There are many
adjustments called for in marriage. What are they? How do married couples face those situations? How do two people find the
fulfillment of their dreams in marriage, the marriage that was begun "in the name of God the Father, God the Son, and God the
Holy Ghost"?

While God has given men and women the ability to bring children into the world, men and women do not possess, nor have they
had automatically bestowed upon them, the wisdom and understanding they need to teach and guide their children in their religious life. Parents will be offered guidance in understanding the
religious needs and capacities of themselves and of their children
as they grow together through the years.

Such illustrations could be multiplied, but it is enough to say that
the Covenant Life Curriculum offers help to those who live in any
kind of family relationship—help designed to develop the faith of
each member of the family and thereby prepare them for life in
the world and in the church. Some educators have thought that the
purpose of family education was to help families that they might
assist the church in its educational work. The basic purpose, however, is that the church may help the family to grow in Christian
knowledge and experience, and in Christlikeness in all things.

The church communicates its faith through its worship and
work. Here the word "church" is used to refer to the congregation
as it assembles for worship, and as it undertakes to carry out its
responsibilities to God and man. The primary purpose of the formal service of worship is that the congregation may adore and bless
the name of God, that it may be instructed and inspired by the

Word and by observing the sacraments of the church. In the church the individuals and families come together in the larger family of God. They hear the Word proclaimed. They partake of Christian fellowship. They receive the sacraments. They go forth into the world as servants of Christ.

The Covenant Life Curriculum is built on the concept that the church should undertake its work as the covenant family. All the boards and agencies of the Presbyterian Church have united in seeking to develop a single over-all approach to the work and worship of the church. The emphasis is upon the worship and work of the particular church. The boards and agencies will supply educational materials and program suggestions for the use of the particular church in order that each congregation may be better prepared to carry out its mission as servant of Christ. The entire congregation will be at work or will engage in study in such areas as witnessing, serving, and facing the problems common to life. As children participate with their elders, and as adults and young people share their views and concerns, the members of the church will become aware of their common responsibilities. Each one can contribute to the understanding and growth of the other.

The church communicates its faith through a planned program of systematic study. This is the activity most commonly associated with Christian education. It includes the school usually held on Sunday morning. In addition to this period for study on Sunday morning there are many other planned activities that educate or offer educational opportunities, such as the vacation church school, fellowship meetings, camps, conferences, retreats, and Bible classes held at other times during the week.

The Covenant Life Curriculum recognizes the vital importance of adult education. The Curriculum Study Committee called the Board's attention to the necessity of offering instruction to adults and of building a curriculum of Christian education that begins with the education of adults. Studies of conditions in the church indicated that a major proportion of adult members were not engaged in a genuine study of the Bible or of the meaning of the Christian life. Christian education materials have generally been created to help children and young people. This is important. But the idea that Christian education should begin with children or young people is erroneous. Education should begin with the instruction and guidance of adults. Adults are officers and leaders of the congregation. Adults shape the nature of communities and cities. Adults are teachers in the church school. Parents are adults. It is imperative that adults should grow in knowledge and in depth of Christian experience—imperative not only for them as adults but in order that children and youth may be nurtured in depth.

"When the educational program of a church is oriented toward children, and not toward adults, there is danger of watering down its teachings generation by generation. The attempt to make the gospel completely intelligible to children or attractive to youth at the expense of its essential nature leads to a superficial understanding of God and a conception of the church as a 'religious club.' Thus the rising generation misunderstands the faith and the great heritage of the church, and people are lost from the educational program before they arrive at the age when they can begin to comprehend the true meaning of the gospel."[4]

The Covenant Life Curriculum was introduced by a special study for adults. An entire year of study has been offered to interpret to adults the educational approach of the Covenant Life Curriculum. Adults have responded in great numbers to this special study. Not only are they enrolled in the church school; they are actively enrolled, studying and taking part in the resulting discussions. A challenging study appeals to adults.

Three Approaches to a Study of the Gospel Message

Three areas of subject matter—the Bible, the church, and the Christian life—are dealt with in the Covenant Life Curriculum.

"The word 'approach' has been chosen as a designation of these areas in order that the dynamic quality of the areas may be continually held in mind. The word 'approach' connotes a combination of subject matter with the teaching-learning process by which the subject matter is communicated."[5]

"The Bible is the basic material of the educational work of the church," as the "Basic Presuppositions" paper states, and therefore is central in the Covenant Life Curriculum. "The Bible is the story of how God comes to men, and it should be allowed to speak its own message. . . . The story of what God has done, what God is doing, what God promises yet to do, is a significant and moving story. Specifically it should be said that the Bible is not a book of heroes to be used as illustrations of the church's moralisms, nor is it a book of science or nature study. . . . The Bible . . . is the spectacles through which a man may see God. Through the pages of Scripture we seek to meet the living Saviour of whom the Scriptures testify."[6]

A further emphasis upon the importance of the use of the Bible is stated as follows: "The Bible is our source of knowledge about Jesus Christ, our Lord and Saviour. Through the Bible the church may listen again and again to the story of God's redeeming love, which called the church into being, and which defines the nature of the church's life and work."[7]

Because of the centrality of the Bible in the curriculum, the first year of the systematic study is in this area, with the emphasis on the wholeness of the Bible. *The Mighty Acts of God,* the first study book, written by A. B. Rhodes, sets forth the way in which God has acted on man's behalf in the drama of redemption. The study shows how God has revealed his redemptive activities during different periods in the history of God's people. This book, planned as an adult study, calls attention to the way the Bible tells its own story. The youth of the church have books upon the same general theme, "The Bible Tells the Story of God's Love." The material for children will use this approach during part of each year.

The second approach is through subject matter relating to the church. Because the church is "witness and instrument of God's revelation,"[8] and is constrained to tell the story entrusted to it, the second year of systematic study deals with the history and life of the church. It shows how God has called a people to enter into covenant with him. The history of the covenant people is marked by failures and rebellion, yet God has persistently called men to repent and return to him. His patience in dealing with them is set forth, as well as the judgment that falls upon those who harden their hearts and resist the Spirit of God. In this study of the church, the Bible remains central in the subject matter of the curriculum.

It was through the story told in the Bible that the church was brought into being. It is through continually retelling this story that the church's life is renewed. How God speaks to his people, how he acts on their behalf, how they respond, what they are summoned to do, and what the church is to believe are made known in Scripture. God's guidance of the church is provided as the Holy Spirit enables the church to perceive and understand the gospel and to bear witness in the world.

The church has a continuous history. The church of today is rooted in the church of history. The story of the church since the days of the New Testament is included in the curriculum. The life and witness of the church will be tested in the light of the Word of God, for the church is formed and reformed by the Word of God. Adults and youth will study subject matter organized around the church as the covenant people of God. Children will be offered material with this approach each year.

The third approach in systematic study is related to the Christian life. The theme might be stated as a study of "Life Under the Lordship of Christ." It is important for believers to know what the nature of the Christian life is. What does the gospel say to man? What is man summoned to become when he is truly related to Christ as a believing person? "Since the church is set in the midst of the tensions of the world today to live as the people of God and to bear witness by its life to God's revelation of himself to man, it is essential that the church turn to an examination of the world in which it lives and toward which the gospel message is directed. Only thus can the church understand the nature of the response to God which the gospel requires."[9]

There are two ways one may approach a study of the Christian faith. One can begin with revelation and proclaim and teach what God has called man to believe and to do. Another approach is through an understanding of the human predicament. As one examines the sinful condition of man and of society he is aware of the importance of hearing what God has to say to man to deliver him from the morass of his sinfulness and to direct him into the way of life demanded of one whose Lord is the Son of God. The predicament of man will be studied as it is, and in the light of the gospel. Thus, again the Word of God will be kept in its central place in the curriculum. "A number of different approaches will be made to this concern of the church. At times there will be study of great scriptural passages that bear most sharply upon the obligations of covenant living—the Ten Commandments, the Old Testament prophets, the words of our Lord, and the epistles to the churches. At times there will be careful analysis of the demands of the Christian faith as a whole—the nature of man's response to God's forgiving love, and the forms this response may take in the various relationships of life. At times the church will be encouraged to start from an examination of situations and problems of today's world and to seek in the Bible the word that God would say to man's need. Always the Covenant Life Curriculum seeks to make clear the fact that the follower of Christ must live under his Lordship and surrender himself to it."[10]

This third approach will be used by adults and youth in the third year of systematic study. In materials prepared for children it will be used in each year of study.

The three approaches to systematic study will be used in succeeding three-year periods. The subject matter for adults will be dealt with as an unfolding spiral. Additional subject matter from different approaches will be presented for study.

One of the strongest elements of the Covenant Life Curriculum is the over-all planning that has taken place in developing the curriculum materials and courses of study that will be offered the church. There is a unity in the curriculum that will bring together the adults, youth, and children of the church as they study great areas of subject matter. The study courses will include material that covers the Bible, theology, church history, Christian ethics, and the work of the church. Authors and editors of curriculum materials will reflect the basic positions described in the report of the Study Committee. Such planning should result in study that leads to a genuine confrontation with God, a deeper understanding of the Word of God, a better-informed church, and a deeper understanding of the life God's people are called to live.

The method of communicating the Christian faith grows out of the nature of the gospel God has revealed. "The educational work of the Christian church finds its motive in the fact that God has revealed himself, finds its message in the revelation itself, and uses methods that are consistent with that revelation of God and of his will."[11] In doing so the church will not overlook the contributions secular education has made to man's understanding of the learning processes and the development of the person. It will select and use as much of the methodology of secular education as is consistent with the nature of the gospel. Christian education is the Christian church seeking to provide nurture in the Christian faith for all people.

The church has been brought into being by the gracious act of God. It has been formed by a series of historical events in which God has intervened in history and has acted on man's behalf. The culmination of these events is found in the life, death, and resurrection of Christ. God confronts man when the story of these events contained in the Bible is told. As man hears the story, he learns of the promise and of the covenant God has made, and, through the Holy Spirit, he responds in faith to the call of God. This call of God is to a way of life experienced in fellowship with him. It becomes the responsibility of the church, therefore, to tell the story God has revealed. The church is to tell the story again and again. To tell it, the church must know it. The teacher and learner must be concerned with the content of revelation.

The Covenant Life Curriculum speaks of a fourfold process of teaching and learning. The process may begin with any one of the four elements but must include all the others.

"The learning process begins with a word that comes from without, demanding to be heard; a given body of truth, which confronts man and to which man must give attention."[12] Opportunity must be given man to hear and understand the word that God has given. The Bible must be allowed to speak its message, and the learner must listen reverently to the word that is spoken. The word speaks of a truth and knowledge beyond the realm of the world and yet dynamic and life-changing when truly heard. "The strange mystery of the gospel is that it is the Spirit of God who speaks and God's Spirit in man who answers, but the Spirit will not intrude if man closes the ears of his heart."[13] To "listen" to the word implies a willingness of heart and mind to hear and to respond to the message contained in the words heard or in the event that occurs.

A second element of the teaching-learning process is the participation and identification of the hearer as he relates himself to the story and events set forth in Scripture. The hearer identifies himself with the persons and experiences related to the Bible story. He realizes that God is speaking to him in ways similar to those in which he spoke to people in the Bible story. The learner struggles with the same issues of faith and life faced by the people of the Bible. The teacher and learner cannot be mere spectators of God's works and acts; they must become involved in those works and acts. "One who teaches or learns by participation finds himself involved in the total Christian enterprise, including the whole biblical story and the life and worship of the local congregation of which he is a part."[14]

A third element of the teaching-learning process is the exploration of the meaning of what has been heard. One analyzes himself, his situation, his world, and his heart as he attempts to understand the demands of the gospel. He examines the nature and mission of the church and its relation to contemporary society. "For this reason the curriculum of Christian education includes not only the data of the Christian faith which have been given us in the Bible and the life of the church, but must also include the significant data about the world in which we live—data which are made available to us through the physical, biological, and social sciences."[15] The data of human sciences are not in themselves the data of the faith, but they are essential to our understanding of its message and to our response.

A fourth element of the teaching-learning process calls for the acceptance of responsibility by the learner. The response to God must be made. The acceptance of responsibility for the Christian message, life, and mission gives evidence of the learner's response to God. One commits himself to the application of the gospel in all phases of life. Learning results in the undertaking of whatever the Holy Spirit calls us to do.

The processes outlined do not necessarily occur in this order. At times the processes may occur simultaneously. The acceptance of responsibility may not occur within the walls of the church. It may, and should, find fruition in the office, in the schoolroom, at home, and everywhere the common life of man is lived.

This educational process is continuous. It implies that curriculum includes the way the church conducts its business and carries out its mission and responds to the gospel. It implies that study may begin with the gospel as revealed, or it may begin with the human predicament and discover what the Bible says about it. It reminds us that the teacher is but a channel through which God speaks and through whom his grace is made known. It affords the teacher ample freedom in his approach to teaching. It constrains him to know Christ and the gospel both intellectually and experientially in order to help others understand it and respond to it.

Christian education uses methods consistent with the nature of the gospel it communicates, consistent with the revelation it has been given.

The Responsibility of the Church for the Education of Its People

It is the concept of the Covenant Life Curriculum that members of the covenant community bear the responsibility for communicating the faith to other persons. This responsibility is individual and corporate.

The writer of the book of Deuteronomy summoned Israel to hearken to the call of God, "to love the Lord thy God with all thine heart, and with all thy soul, and with all thy might." Then followed the charge of responsibility: "And these words, which I command thee this day, shall be in thine heart: and thou shalt teach them diligently unto thy children."[16] The covenant people were responsible for teaching the story of God's deliverance of Israel from bondage, and for teaching the laws and commandments they had received at Mount Sinai.

Jesus, the Son of God, by his ministry established the importance of teaching. He called men to be his disciples. He prepared them for their ministry. He interpreted to them the depth of the meaning of many Old Testament passages and concepts. He taught individuals as he walked along the way, sat in the home of friends, drank water from an ancient well to which a thirsty woman had come, spoke to the multitudes by the sea, expounded the message of the Kingdom to the disciples who came up into the mountains with him, and explained to two disciples on the road to Emmaus the relation of the Old Testament to the events men had witnessed in Jerusalem. As Jesus was about to ascend into heaven, he said, "Go . . . and make disciples of all nations . . . teaching them to observe all that I have commanded you."[17]

The very nature of discipleship and of the gospel calls upon all believers to communicate it to others.

In Summary

The Covenant Life Curriculum gathers up the basic elements of Christian education as reflected in the history of the early church, in the writings of John Calvin and John Knox, and in the history of the Presbyterian Church in the United States. At the same time it specifically reflects the insights of modern Bible scholars, theologians, educators, and students of social sciences.

The early Christians recognized the importance of education. New converts were given thorough instruction in the meaning of the gospel. Children of believers were instructed in the doctrines of the church before they were allowed to receive the sacrament of the Lord's Supper. For hundreds of years all Christians were urged to read and understand the Scriptures.

The education of believers was a central factor in Calvin's ministry. Through his extensive writings, particularly the *Institutes of the Christian Religion,* he encouraged sound learning and instruction in the Christian faith. His expositions of the Scriptures, through his preaching-teaching ministry, his commentaries, and his sermons, enabled those who were interested in the Word of God to understand it. He prepared a catechism for children and young people that they might be instructed in the doctrines of the Christian community. He taught the clergy and officers of the church and expected them to teach their members. Calvin's concepts of nurture reflected an emphasis upon reform of conduct as well as of doctrine. The Scriptures were relevant to the political, moral, and social conditions that prevailed in Geneva. Calvin's scheme of education reflected his belief that children and youth should be offered a sound education, and that in all education—and this included education in the college and university—God was to be at the center.

John Knox, having been instructed by Calvin, advocated essentially the same concepts of Christian education. More than did Calvin, however, Knox emphasized the importance of Bible study for adults. His letter to the leaders of the Reformation in Scotland described a pattern of study strikingly similar to patterns of group discussion in Bible classes today. One of the most important concepts of Christian education in Knox's writings, a concept still reflected in the Church of Scotland, was the instruction of children by their parents. Family worship and the religious training parents gave their children were marks of Knox's ministry that have had a continuing influence upon Scotland and people of Scottish descent.

The distinguishing characteristics of Christian education in the Presbyterian Church have undergone many changes. There has been an emphasis upon the mastery of the content of the Bible and of the Confession of Faith and the catechisms. The curriculum provided for the church by the Board of Christian Education has always included teaching materials on the life and work of the church. Missions, evangelism, and stewardship have been given special emphasis. In recent years the curriculum has reflected a deep concern for the understanding of the person, of how learning takes place, and of the importance of the method by which the Christian faith is communicated. There has been a growing concern over the moral and ethical implications of the gospel. Greater attention has been given to the importance of the family as the first school of religious instruction.

The Covenant Life Curriculum reflects the essential concepts of Christian education found in its historic origins. It is developed upon the bases set forth in the original paper entitled "Basic Presuppositions and Guiding Principles for the Educational Work of the Church." Thus it attempts to bring into the educational work of the church the best insights of theologians, Bible scholars, educators, and churchmen of today.

The Covenant Life Curriculum gives promise of bringing genuine renewal to the church. It presents a dynamic approach to study, an approach that should lead men into a genuine confrontation with God. Experience with God will undoubtedly be deepened. Christians will be better informed concerning the content of faith and the history of the church. Christians will be called upon to enter into the struggles of a society that cries out for justice, freedom, and dignity. The organized church will give less consideration to its institutional patterns of life and greater consideration to its relationships with God and man in the name of Christ. The family will receive help in discovering the meaning of the gospel, in finding strength and inspiration to live in covenant relationship with one another and with the families of the world. The church will be more concerned about drawing into its fellowship, and into covenant relationship with God, all people, regardless of class, color, or condition, and less concerned about a form of church life that has become too much like the life of a secular world.

Whatever happens through the Covenant Life Curriculum will be the result of the work of God. The Holy Spirit will work when he will and howsoever he will in order that Christ may be known and served as Redeemer and King.

Acknowledgments

2 CALVIN AND CHRISTIAN EDUCATION

1. *Calvin: Institutes of the Christian Religion,* edited by John T. McNeill (Philadelphia: The Westminster Press, 1960), p. 9.
2. Theodore Beza, *The Life of John Calvin* (Philadelphia: J. Whetham, 1836), p. 12.
3. John Calvin, *Institutes of the Christian Religion,* translated by John Allen (Philadelphia: The Westminster Press, 1936), Vol. I, Book I, Ch. VII, p. 85.
4. *Ibid.,* pp. 88-89.
5. *Ibid.,* p. 90.
6. A. Mitchell Hunter, *The Teaching of Calvin* (Glasgow: Maclehose, Jackson & Co., 1920), p. 61.
7. *Ibid.,* p. 64.
8. *Ibid.,* p. 83.
9. Felix Bungener, *Calvin: His Life, His Labours, and His Writings,* translated from the French (Edinburgh: T. & T. Clark, 1863), p. 282.
10. John Calvin, *Tracts Containing Treatises on the Sacraments . . .,* translated by Henry Beveridge (Edinburgh: Calvin Translation Society, 1869), pp. 82-83.
11. *Ibid.,* p. 83.
12. *Ibid.,* p. 37.
13. *Ibid.,* p. 115.
14. *Ibid.,* pp. 115-116.
15. *Ibid.,* p. 116.
16. *Ibid.,* p. 117.
17. Samuel Dunn, *Christian Theology by John Calvin. Selected and Systematically Arranged with A Life of the Author* (London: Tegg & Son, 1837), p. 299.
18. *Ibid.*
19. *Ibid.,* p. 302.
20. *Ibid.,* p. 307.
21. *Ibid.,* pp. 308-309.
22. *Ibid.,* p. 309.

23. Calvin, *Institutes*, Vol. I, Book III, Ch. VII, p. 751.
24. Hunter, *op. cit.*, p. 189.
25. *Ibid.*, pp. 189-190. (Quoted phrases from Calvin's *Institutes*, Book IV, Ch. XX, Pars. 2, 3.)
26. Calvin, *Institutes*, Vol. I, p. 25.
27. I Corinthians 13:1 (King James Version).
28. Bungener, *op. cit.*, p. 113.
29. Hunter, *op. cit.*, pp. 291, 294-295.
30. *Ibid.*, p. 297.

3 JOHN KNOX AND CHRISTIAN EDUCATION

1. Alexander F. Mitchell, *The Scottish Reformation* (Edinburgh: William Blackwood and Sons, 1900), p. 1.
2. *Ibid.*, p. 12.
3. *John Knox's History of the Reformation in Scotland,* edited by William Croft Dickinson (New York: Philosophical Library, 1950), Vol. I, p. 69.
4. P. Hume Brown, *John Knox: A Biography* (London: Adam and Charles Black, 1895), Vol. II, p. 288.
5. James Stalker, *John Knox: His Ideas and Ideals* (London: Hodder and Stoughton, 1904), p. 129.
6. *Ibid.*, p. 132.
7. Dickinson, ed., *op. cit.*, Vol. II, p. 267.
8. Lord Eustace Percy, *John Knox* (London: Hodder and Stoughton, n.d.), p. 60.
9. *Ibid.*, p. 61.
10. David Hoy Fleming, *The Reformation in Scotland: Causes, Characteristics, Consequences* (London: Hodder and Stoughton, 1910), p. 222. (Quoted phrase from *Catholic Dictionary*, p. 82.)
11. *Ibid.*, p. 223. (Quoted phrase, *ibid.*)
12. From "Soliloquy of the Spanish Cloister," in *The Complete Poetic and Dramatic Works of Robert Browning* (Boston: Houghton Mifflin Company, 1895), p. 168.
13. Dickinson, ed., *op. cit.*, Vol. II, p. 18.
14. James Stalker, *op. cit.*, pp. 140-141.
15. *Ibid.*, p. 142.
16. James S. McEwen, *The Faith of John Knox* (London: Lutterworth Press, 1961), p. 41.
17. John Knox, *The History of the Reformation of Religion in Scotland,* edited by Cuthbert Lennox (Edinburgh: Andrew Melrose, 1905), p. 383.
18. P. Hume Brown, *John Knox: A Biography* (London: Adam and Charles Black, 1895), Vol. II, pp. 146-147.
19. *Ibid.*, pp. 147-148.
20. *Ibid.*, p. 148. (Lines of verse from William Wordsworth, "Resolu-

tion and Independence.")
21. *The Works of John Knox,* edited by David Laing (Edinburgh: Printed for the Wodrow Society, 1848), Vol. II, p. 114.
22. *Ibid.,* p. 115.
23. Dickinson, *op. cit.,* Vol. I, p. 165.
24. *Ibid.,* p. 174.

4 THE ROAD WE HAVE TRAVELED

1. *The Book of Church Order* (revised 1961), §27-6(2).
2. Minutes of the General Assembly, 1866, p. 37.
3. Ernest Trice Thompson, *The Spirituality of the Church* (Richmond: John Knox Press, 1961), p. 20.
4. *Ibid.,* p. 21.
5. *Ibid.,* p. 23.
6. *Ibid.,* pp. 24-25.
7. Minutes of the General Assembly, 1875, p. 43.
8. Minutes of the General Assembly, 1885, p. 408.
9. Minutes of the General Assembly, 1886, p. 45.
10. Minutes of the General Assembly, 1894, p. 238.
11. Minutes of the General Assembly, 1904, p. 72.
12. Minutes of the General Assembly, 1865, pp. 370-371.

5 COVENANT LIFE CURRICULUM

1. "Basic Presuppositions and Guiding Principles" (Richmond: Board of Christian Education, Presbyterian Church, U. S., 1960), p. 5.
2. *Ibid.*
3. *Education for Covenant Living* (Richmond: Board of Christian Education, Presbyterian Church, U. S., 1962), p. 25.
4. "Basic Presuppositions and Guiding Principles," p. 8.
5. "Three Approaches into the Christian Faith to Be Used in the Educational Work of the Church," p. 4.
6. "Basic Presuppositions and Guiding Principles," p. 6.
7. "Three Approaches into the Christian Faith," p. 5.
8. *Ibid.*
9. *Ibid.*
10. *Ibid.,* p. 6.
11. "Basic Presuppositions and Guiding Principles," p. 5.
12. "The Teaching-Learning Process to Be Used in the Educational Work of the Church" (Richmond: Board of Christian Education, Presbyterian Church, U. S., 1961), p. 6.
13. *Ibid.*
14. *Ibid.,* p. 7.
15. *Ibid.*
16. Deuteronomy 6:5-7 (King James Version).
17. Matthew 28:18 (Revised Standard Version).